Wildy Pra

Child Care and Protection
Law and Practice

Barbara Mitchels, LLB, Ph.D, UKRC, FBACP, Children Panel Solicitor

with

Helen James, RCCYP, CQSW, FRSA, ISW Consultant and Children's Guardian

Fourth Edition

Wildy, Simmonds and Hill Publishing 2009

© 2009 Wildy, Simmonds & Hill Publishing

Fourth edition first published in Great Britain 2009 by Wildy, Simmonds & Hill Publishing

Website: www.wildy.com

Mitchels, Barbara

Child care protection law and practice – 4th ed (Wildy Practice Guides series)

1 Children - legal status, laws, etc - England

2 Children - legal status, laws, etc - Wales

I Title II James, Helen

ISBN 9780854900381

Printed and bound in Great Britain

Preface

Child care and protection in England is a vast and dynamic area of law and practice. We cannot cover everything here, but we hope this book provides an overview and practical guide through the maze of the Children Act 1989 and subsequent child protection legislation, guidance and case law. Since the last edition in 2001 there have been substantial developments in legislation and practice. This edition covers new material, including *Every Child Matters* and its subsequent legislation and guidance, the Children Act 2004, parts of the Adoption and Children Act 2002, the Children and Adoption Act 2006, and the *Public Law Outline* (PLO). Our discussion of inter-agency co-operation in child protection practice is based upon the revised edition of *Working Together to Safeguard Children* (2006). We hope that the new private law provisions for warnings, enforcement and 'contact activity directions', with the current emphasis on family mediation, will prove helpful in the resolution of contact difficulties, for the benefit of children and their families.

The courts have been greatly concerned about delays in hearing cases within the family court system. The first attempt at grasping the nettle was an interim *Protocol for Judicial Case Management* issued in 2003. This is now replaced by the *Public Law Outline*, which was issued as *Practice Direction: Guide to Case Management in Public Law Proceedings* by the President of the Family Division, and operative from 1 April 2008.

New developments have not all been positive. The PLO expects local authorities to carry out core assessments before issuing s 31 applications. This has come at a very difficult time, when resources may be limited. Local authorities are still endeavouring to implement all the new provisions generated by *Every Child Matters*. The government has also significantly raised the amount that local authorities have to pay in court fees in care matters, and there is a risk that local authorities may now delay in, or even be deterred from issuing child protection proceedings.

The courts are doing their best to implement the PLO and avoid delays in the judicial process, but are contending with a lack of funding. Resources within CAFCASS are similarly under strain and there are limitations on the availability of children's guardians in specified proceedings, with some child protection hearings taking place without the presence of a children's guardian, yet CAFCASS no longer makes use of many experienced self-employed children's guardians formerly contracted. There are also ongoing issues between CAFCASS and the courts about the current judicial power to make a named appointment of a children's guardian in care matters.

The public funding (legal aid) system is experiencing financial constraints. The Legal Services Commission has revised its franchise contracts with lawyers, effectively reducing the funding available for child protection cases, and as a result, many experienced Children Panel practitioners have abandoned that area of legal practice.

After the sad death of Victoria Climbie in 2000, Lord Laming's Inquiry (2003) made specific recommendations regarding child protection practice. In 2007/8, Home Office data show that 55 children were killed by their parents or someone known to the child. Following the tragic death of Baby P in 2007, the government published Lord Laming's review of the implementation of his earlier recommendations – *The Protection of Children in England* (12 March 2009), which highlights urgent need for improvement.

For all the reasons outlined above, we are greatly concerned about the welfare of children who are at risk. Our concern is shared by the many of the judiciary, lawyers, children's guardians and social workers with whom we work.

Practitioners who want to take effective action to help children, families and local authorities also need to understand the work and concerns of social services, police, health practitioners and other agencies. The qualification for membership of the Children Panel (which covers legal representation of children, adults and local authorities) includes a wide range of relevant sociological, psychological, medical and practice issues.

Advocacy and giving evidence as a professional or expert witness can seem daunting, but practitioners can become confident in court through careful case preparation and by developing an understanding of court procedures and the mutual expectations of courts and professional witnesses, so we have provided examples and insights from practice.

This book provides brief notes on the salient points in child care and protection law and practice as it operates in England. Other jurisdictions are covered only where specifically mentioned. It is always difficult to decide what to include or omit, and we try to provide as many pointers as we can to useful cases, resources and reference works. Lawyers and practitioners from other disciplines working with children should meet together as often as they can to share their ideas and experience, debate thorny issues, tackle challenges and celebrate success. We, too, welcome ideas and feedback, and will use information that we acquire from practitioners to improve subsequent editions.

Please interpret our use of 'he' and 'she', for variety, to include either gender, where relevant and appropriate.

Despite all the current challenges, specialism in this area of law remains very rewarding, and necessary. We both feel privileged to work in our different ways with children and their families, and with other people actively involved in child care and protection.

Barbara Mitchels and Helen James, 6 April 2009

Acknowledgments

Barbara gives grateful thanks to Helen James, Children's Guardian and Independent Social Work Consultant for her assistance with the book, and in particular her thoughts relating to recent developments in *Every Child Matters*, care planning and assessments and for her wisdom, experience, support, and sense of humour as a colleague on family work, mediations, and course facilitation over the years, particularly in our Children Panel and child protection training.

Many thanks to all those who have given their permission to include quotations, references and materials, and our particular appreciation to David Lane, Senior Lecturer in Childhood Studies at Liverpool John Moore's University, for his ideas, encouragement, and very helpful comments on the text.

We have really appreciated the experience and help of Andrew Riddoch and Brian Hill from Wildy's for their time and patience in working with us to design this book which is the first of this series.

Thank you, too, for the advice and help of the many professionals, volunteers, children and families over the years with whom we have worked. They were often better sources of information and practice improvement than any law book!

Finally, especial thanks to our own families, for their tolerance, patience and fortifying cups of coffee whilst this was being written!

Barbara and Helen

Contents

1 Glossary and Legislative Framework

1.1 Glossary of basic definitions

Interpretations of many terms used within the Children Act 1989 are given in s 105. The source of definitions created by other sections, other Acts or by case law and other sources are cited. Unless otherwise stated, sections cited are from the Children Act 1989 (CA 1989).

Adoption agency

Defined in s 2(1) of the Adoption and Children Act 2002 and includes local authorities and approved adoption organisations. Their work is regulated by the Adoption Agencies Regulations 2005, SI 2005/389 and in Wales, the Adoption Agencies (Wales) Regulations 2002/1313.

Authorised person

(a) In care and supervision proceedings, and in child assessment orders, this means the NSPCC or its officers, under ss 31(9) and 43(13) CA 1989. A person (other than a local authority) may be authorised by order of the Secretary of State to bring proceedings under s 31 CA 1989 for a care or supervision order, but no one has been so authorised;

(b) in emergency protection orders, proceedings may be brought by an 'authorised officer' of the local authority, an 'authorised person' (as defined in (a) above), a 'designated' police officer or 'any other person'; see ss 31(9) and 44 CA 1989.

Authority

The local authority of a geographical area, including county councils, district councils, unitary authorities in England and Wales, Welsh county councils and Welsh county borough councils.

Care order

An order made under s 31(1)(a) CA 1989, placing a child in the care of a local authority. By s 31(11), this includes an interim care order made under s 38. By s 105, any reference to a child who is in the care of an authority is a reference to a child who is in their care by virtue of a care order.

Child

A person under the age of 18.

Child assessment order

An order under s 43 CA 1989 to produce the child and to comply with the court's directions relating to the assessment of the child. There are restrictions on keeping the child away from home under this section.

Child in care

A child in the care of a local authority pursuant to an order made under s 31(1)(a) CA 1989 or an interim order made under s 38 CA 1989.

Child in need

Under s 17 CA 1989, 'a child is taken to be in need if:

(a)   he is unlikely to achieve or maintain, or to have the opportunity of achieving or maintaining, a reasonable standard of health or development without the provision for him of services by a local authority;

(b)   his health or development is likely to be significantly impaired or further impaired, without the provision for him of such services; or he is disabled.'

(*Also, see Assessing Children in Need and their Families (2000) and Framework For the Assessment of Children in Need and Their Families (2000).*)

Child minder

Defined in s 71 CA 1989 as a person who looks after one or more children under the age of eight, for reward; for total period(s) exceeding two hours in any one day. A person is not deemed to provide day care for children unless the total period(s) during which the children are looked after exceeds two hours in any day.

Child of the family

In relation to the parties to a marriage, means (a) a child of both of those parties, (b) any other child, not being a child who is placed with those parties by a local authority or voluntary organisation, who has been treated by both of those parties as a child of their family.'

Child looked after by a local authority

A child who is in the care of a local authority by virtue of a care order, or provided with accommodation by a local authority.

Child provided with accommodation by a local authority

A child who is provided with accommodation by a local authority in the exercise of its functions which stand referred to their social services committee under the Local Authorities Social Services Act 1970 (includes children in what was previously called 'voluntary care').

Children's home

Defined in s 63 CA 1989 as a home which usually provides or is intended to provide care and accommodation wholly or mainly for more than three children at any one time. Obviously, many homes contain three or more children and the section lists several exceptions, including the homes of parents, relatives, or those with parental responsibility for the children in question.

Community home

Defined in s 53 CA 1989 and may be (a) a home provided, equipped and maintained by a local authority, or (b) provided by a voluntary organisation but in respect of which ... the management, equipment and maintenance of the home shall be the responsibility of the local authority; ... or the responsibility of the voluntary organisation'.

Contact order

Defined in s 8(1) CA 1989 as 'an order requiring the person with whom a child lives, or is to live, to allow the child to visit or stay with the person named in the order, or for that person and the *child otherwise to have contact with each other*'.

Development

Defined in s 31(9) CA 1989 as physical, intellectual, emotional, social or behavioural development.

Disabled Defined in s 17(11) CA 1989 and 'in relation to a child, means a child who is blind, deaf, or dumb or who suffers from mental disorder of any kind or who is substantially and permanently handicapped by illness, injury or congenital deformity or such other disability as may be prescribed.

Education Supervision Order An order under s 36(1) CA 1989, putting the child with respect to whom the order is made under the supervision of a designated local education authority

Emergency Protection Order Under s 44 CA 1989, this order:

'(a) operates as a direction to any person ... in a position to do so to comply with any request to produce the child ...

(b) authorises:

the removal of a child to accommodation provided by or on behalf of the applicant, and his being kept there; or the prevention of the child's removal from any hospital or other place in which he was being accommodated immediately before the making of the order; and

(c) gives the applicant parental responsibility for the child.'

(But also note – the exercise of parental responsibility under this order has limitations; see below, Chapter 5.)

Family Assistance Order

An order made under s 16 CA 1989 appointing a probation officer or an officer of the local authority to advise, assist and (where appropriate) befriend any person named in the order for a period of six months or less. Named persons may include parents, guardians, those with whom the child lives, or the child himself.

Family proceedings

In the Family Proceedings Court, all proceedings are treated as 'family proceedings' under s 92(2).

However, in other courts, 'family proceedings' are defined in s 8(3) and (4) as including any proceedings:

(a) under the inherent jurisdiction of the High Court in relation to children, including wardship but not applications for leave under s 100(3);

(b) under Pts I, II and IV of the Act; the Matrimonial Causes Act 1973; the Adoption Act 1976; the Domestic Proceedings and Magistrates' Courts Act 1978; Pt III of the Matrimonial and Family Law Act 1996; also under ss 11 and 12 of the Crime and Disorder Act 1998;

(c) under s 30(8) of the Human Fertilisation and Embryology Act 1990, proceedings under s 30 of that Act are included.

(Note that the definitions in s 8(3) and 8(4) do not include applications for emergency protection orders, child assessment orders or recovery orders.)

Guardian

Means a guardian appointed under s 5 of the Act for the child, but not for the child's estate.

Children's Guardian

An officer of the court with a duty to report to the court on the best course to be taken in the interests of the child. See ss 41-42 CA 1989, and the Children Act Guidance Vol 7.

Harm

Defined in s 31(9) CA 1989, meaning the ill treatment or the impairment of health or development. Where the question of whether the harm is significant or not turns on the child's health and development, his health or development shall be compared with that which could be reasonably expected of a similar child, s 31(10).

Health

Includes physical and mental health.

Hospital

Any health service hospital, and accommodation provided by the local authority and used as a hospital. It does not include special hospitals, which are those for people detained under the Mental Health Act 1983, providing secure hospital accommodation.

Ill treatment

Defined in s 31(9) CA 1989 and includes sexual abuse and forms of ill treatment which are not physical.

Kinship care

Care for a child by family members or friends of the family. Kinship care may be arranged privately, on a voluntary basis, or as part of a care plan in the context of a care order.

Local authority

A council of a county, a metropolitan district, a London borough, or the Common Council of the City of London; in Scotland, it means a local authority under Social Work (Scotland) Act 1968, s 12.

Local authority foster parent

Any person with whom a child has been placed by a local authority under s 23(2)(a) CA 1989. Local authority foster parents may include a family; a relative of the child; or any other suitable person.

Local housing authority

Defined in the Housing Act 1944, meaning the district council; a London borough council; the Common Council of the City of London; or Council of the Isles of Scilly.

Parent

The natural (birth) mother or father of a child, whether or not they are married to each other at the time of the birth or of conception. The Children Act 1989, when it says 'parent', means the birth parents of a child, including therefore natural fathers without parental responsibility. Where it intends to mean 'a parent with parental responsibility', it says so specifically.

Parent (in relation to adoption)

Under the Adoption and Children Act 2002, the consent of each 'parent or guardian of the child' must be obtained for adoption or dispensed with by the court. S 52(6)of that Act defines 'parent' as 'a parent having parental responsibility for the child…'

Family Procedure (Adoption) Rules 2005, SI 2005/2795, rule 23 for applicants and respondents to applications.

Once a child has been adopted, their birth parents are no longer legally 'parents' of the child. Former parents would therefore need leave to apply for s 8 orders after adoption.

Parent with Parental Responsibility

All mothers have parental responsibility for children born to them.

Fathers also have parental responsibility for their child if they married their child's mother before or after the child's birth.

The father of a child who is not married to the mother is able to acquire parental responsibility in various ways under the Children Act 1989. This term therefore excludes the child's natural birth father of a child who has not yet acquired parental responsibility under the Act. See Chapter 3.

Parental responsibility

Defined in s 3 CA 1989 and includes all the rights, duties, powers, responsibilities and authority which by law a parent of a child has in relation to the child and his property. It can be acquired by unmarried fathers in respect of their child by registration of the birth with the mother after 1 December 2003, court order, or by a parental responsibility agreement under the Children Act, and by others through residence or guardianship orders, or by a local authority under a care order. Parental responsibility can be shared with others. It ceases when the child reaches 18, on adoption, death, or cessation of the care order. See Chapter 3 for discussion.

Parental responsibility agreement

Defined in s 4(1) CA 1989 as an agreement between the father and mother of a child providing for the father to have parental responsibility for the child (a father married to the mother of their child at the time of the birth will automatically have parental responsibility for that child, but a father not so married will not). Format for the agreement is set out in the Parental Responsibility Agreement Regulations 1991, SI 1991/1478, as amended by SI 1994/3157. See chapter 3.

Private fostering

See s 66 CA 1989: to 'foster a child privately' means looking after a child under the age of 16 (or if disabled, 18), caring and providing accommodation for him or her; by someone who is not the child's parent, relative, or who has parental responsibility for the child.

Private Law Outline

> Guidance issued by the President of the Family Division on the preparation, timetabling and presentation of private law family cases.
>
> (*See President's Guidance: The Private Law Programme (2004) and President's Guidance: Adoption Proceedings. Intercountry Adoption Centres (2007)*)

Prohibited steps order

> Defined in s 8(1) CA 1989. Means an order that no step which could be taken by a parent in meeting his parental responsibility for a child, and which is of a kind specified in the order, shall be taken by any person without the consent of the court.

Public Law Outline

> Referred to colloquially in court as 'the PLO', the Public Law Outline was issued as Practice Direction: Guide to Case Management in Public Law Proceedings by the President of the Family Division, and operative from 1 April 2008. It provides guidance on how family proceedings should be prepared, timetabled and presented in court, including expert evidence.

Registered children's home

> Defined in s 63 CA 1989 as a home, registered under the Act, which provides (or usually provides or is intended to provide) care and accommodation wholly or mainly for more than three children, who are not siblings with respect to each other, at any one time. Section 63 CA 1989 provides a number of exceptions to the category of children's homes.

Relative

> In relation to a child, this means a grandparent, brother, sister, uncle or aunt (whether of the full blood or of the half blood or by affinity) or step-parent.

Residence order

> An order under s 8(1) CA 1989 settling the arrangements to be made as to the person with whom a child is to live.

Responsible person

> Defined in Sch 3, para 1 CA 1989. In relation to a supervised child, it means:
>
> (a) any person who has parental responsibility for the child; and
>
> (b) any other person with whom the child is living.

Service

> In relation to any provision made under Part III CA 1989 (local authority support for children and families), this means any facility.

Special educational needs

These arise when there is a learning difficulty which calls for special educational provision to be made. The Education Act 1981, s 1(1) sets out the meaning of 'learning difficulty'.

Specific Issue Order

An order under s 8(1) CA 1989 giving directions for the purpose of determining a specific issue which has arisen, or which may arise, in connection with any aspect of parental responsibility for a child.

Supervision Order

An order under s 31(1) (b) and (except where express provision to the contrary is made) includes an interim supervision order made under s 38 CA 1989.

Supervised child/supervisor

In relation to a supervision order or an education supervision order, these mean respectively the child who is (or is to be) under supervision and the person under whose supervision he is (or is to be) by virtue of the order.

Upbringing

In relation to any child, this includes the care of the child but not his maintenance.

Voluntary home

Means any home or other institution providing care and accommodation for children which is carried on by a voluntary organisation, with certain exceptions set out in s 60 CA 1989.

Voluntary organisation

Means a body (other than a public or local authority) whose activities are not carried on for profit.

1.2 Orders available under the Children Act 1989

Order	*Section*	*Maximum duration**
Parental Responsibility	4	Age 18
Guardianship	5	Age 18
Residence	8	Age 16 (18 in exceptional circumstances)
Contact	8	Age 16 (18 in exceptional circumstances)
Prohibited Steps	8	Age 16 (18 in exceptional circumstances)
Specific Issue	8	Age 16 (18 in exceptional circumstances)

Special Guardianship Order	14A	Age 18 (or earlier revocation)
Family Assistance Order	16	Six months
Care order	31	Age 18
Interim Care Order	38	First, not more than eight weeks; remainder, maximum four weeks
Supervision Order	31	Age 18; one year, may be extended to maximum total three years
Care Contact Order	34	For duration of care order
Education Supervision Order	36	One year; repeatedly extensible for three years. Ceases at age 16
Child assessment	43	Seven days
Emergency protection	44	Eight days; extensible for further seven days

* These orders may be brought to an end by court order, variation or discharge and subject to additional provisions. For details, please refer to the relevant chapter.

1.3 Introduction to the Children Act 1989

The Children Act 1989 came into force on 19 October 1991, containing 108 sections and 15 Schedules, and was accompanied by the Family Proceedings Courts (Children Act 1989) Rules 1991 SI 1991/1395; the Family Proceedings (Children) Rules 1991 SI 1991/910; and several volumes of *Guidance and Regulations* (listed below, 1.5).

The Children Act created a new unified court system consisting of three tiers: the High Court, the county court and the family proceedings court, each of which have concurrent jurisdiction and powers. Appeals from the family proceedings court lie to the county court and High Court to the Court of Appeal and the House of Lords. Cases may move up or down the tiers, transfers therefore being easier. The avoidance of delay is one of the underlying principles of the Children Act 1989. This Act, along with its subsidiary rules, created a new system of directions hearings to enable the courts to take firmer control of the timing of cases, admission of evidence and administrative matters.

The Children Act 1989 encourages families to stay together, imposing a duty on local authorities to provide services for children in need and their families, to reduce the necessity for children to be looked after away from home, and for child protection proceedings. Unless the criteria for the making of care or supervision orders are met, an order cannot be made. the courts, if concerned about the welfare of a child, may order a local authority to investigate the child's circumstances, but the courts have no power of their own volition to order a child into the care of a local authority.

The Children Act 1989 introduced a new concept of parental responsibility, which unmarried fathers may gain in relation to their children, and accessible to others, for example, grandparents or step-parents in conjunction with residence orders. It also creates orders governing aspects of a child's life, that is, contact with others; residence; and resolution of disputed aspects of child care – prohibited steps (forbidding actions) and specific issues (permitting actions to take place).

The powers of the police to act in a child's interests to remove and/or retain a child away from home are now limited to 72 hours.

The principles behind the Children Act 1989 and its guidance are that children are people whose rights are to be respected, not just 'objects of concern', and that children should wherever possible remain with their families, helped if necessary by provision of services, provided that their welfare is safeguarded. An atmosphere of negotiation and cooperation between professionals is encouraged. The welfare of the child is paramount, and, in the field of child care and protection, professionals are expected to work together in a non-adversarial way for the benefit of the child.

Section 6 of the Human Rights Act 1998 makes it unlawful for public authorities to act in ways incompatible with the Convention rights. This includes courts, tribunals and local authorities, including both acts and omissions (s 6). Those affected may bring proceedings or rely on the Convention (s 7) by way of an appeal, complaint or judicial review.

1.4 Introduction to *Every Child Matters* and the Children Act 2004

Every Child Matters: Change for Children, a green paper setting out the Government's vision for children's services, was published in September 2003, and the recommended changes are now being implemented through the Children Act 2004.

In Scotland, *It's Everyone's Job to Make Sure that I'm Alright*, the report of the Child Protection Audit Review carried out across Scotland, was published in November 2002, and a programme of reforms are now being implemented, see for example the Commissioner for Children and Young People (Scotland) Act 2003), *Protecting Children and Young People: The Charter* (Scottish Executive (2004a)), and *Protecting Children and Young People: The Framework for Standards*, (Scottish Executive (2004b)).

The Children Act 2004 creates a structure of duties and responsibility shared between national government, local government, and non-governmental organisations to provide 'children's services'. For further details of the provisions for implementation see the *Children Act 2004 (Children's Services) Regulations 2005 SI 2005/1972*.

Under these provisions, local Authorities are empowered to set up arrangements for co-operation among local partners: district councils, police, probation service, youth offending teams, strategic health authorities, primary care trusts, Connexions, and the Learning and Skills Council. These are all implemented through the Children's Trust, with participation by schools, GP practices, culture, sports and play organisations and the voluntary and community sector.

These organisations should have clear policies and procedures for co-operation in child protection, including procedures for information sharing for the benefit of the child or young person.

The Children Act 1989 places a statutory duty on health, education and other services to help the local authority in carrying out its functions under the CA 1989 (similar provisions exist in the Children (Scotland) Act 1995 and *Protecting Children – A shared responsibility: Guidance on Inter-Agency Co-operation* (1998). There is a statutory duty to work together, including information sharing, in conducting initial investigations of children who may be in need or subject to abuse and in the more detailed core assessments carried out under s 47 of the CA 1989. For details of the assessment process see also *Framework for Assessment of Children in Need and their Families* (2000).

The *Every Child Matters* website provides a list of online guidance documents. See, for example, *Working Together to Safeguard Children: A guide to Inter-Agency Working to Safeguard and Promote the Welfare of Children*, (2006) and its supporting materials, all available from the *Every Child Matters* website http://www.everychildmatters.gov.uk. Other useful references are *Information Sharing – A Practitioner's Guide* (2006); *What to do if you are worried that a child is being abused* (2006); and *Confidentiality: NHS Code of Practice* (2003).

2 Principles Underlying the Children Act 1989

2.1 Paramountcy of the welfare of the child

The Children Act 1989 (CA 1989) commences with a clear direction in s 1(1) that: When a court determines any question with respect to:

(a) the upbringing of a child; or

(b) the administration of a child's property or the application of any income arising from it,

the child's welfare shall be the paramount consideration.

The child's welfare is not always easy to determine, and so the CA 1989 sets out a list of criteria in s 1(3), known as the 'welfare checklist'. It is primarily intended as an aide-memoire, particularly useful for judges, children's guardians, professional and expert witnesses, but the court must have regard to it when considering an application to vary or discharge an order under Pt IV of the Children Act (a child protection order), a special guardianship order, or a contested s 8 order for contact, residence, specific issue or prohibited steps, and magistrates should always refer to the check list when considering their findings of fact and reasons for their decisions.

The welfare checklist is not compulsory in other circumstances, but it is always useful for practitioners to consider it. If experts refer to these criteria whilst writing their reports, they will ensure that they are complying with the principles of the Act.

2.1.1 The welfare checklist

(a) The ascertainable wishes and feelings of the child concerned (considered in the light of his age and understanding).

(b) His physical, emotional and educational needs.

(c) The likely effect on him of any change in his circumstances.

(d) His age, sex, background and any characteristics of his which the court considers relevant.

(e) Any harm which he is suffering or which he is at risk of suffering.

(f) How capable each of his parents, and any other person in relation to whom the court considers the question to be relevant, is of
meeting his needs.

(g) The range of powers available to the court under this Act in the
proceedings in question.

There have been a number of cases in which the welfare checklist
has been discussed. The welfare checklist has been held irrelevant
in applications for leave to seek a s 8 order, where the criteria in s
10(9) apply. These are not substantive hearings under the Act (see
North Yorkshire CC v G [1993] 2 FLR 732). However, if the child is
the applicant for leave, then s 10(9) does not apply and the welfare
principle is operative (*Re C (A Minor)* [1994] 1 FLR. 96).

The children's guardian most often advises the court on the child's
welfare in cases under Pt IV of the Act; see below, 15.1. There is an
expectation that a children's guardian will be appointed in 'specified
proceedings', as defined in s 41 CA 1989.

In private law cases (those between individuals as opposed to those
involving State intervention in a family's life), in proceedings that are
not 'specified proceedings' listed in s 41 CA 1989, the court may ask
the children and family reporter/court welfare officer to investigate the
child's circumstances and to report back to the court the child's wishes
and feelings, also advising the court on the best way to safeguard the
child's welfare.

The court should be alert to any unusual circumstances or factors
of concern in private law cases, even if the parties themselves are in
agreement. The court may, where there is a concern, make a direction
to the local authority to investigate the child's circumstances under
s 37 of the Children Act 1989 and appoint a children's guardian to
safeguard the welfare of the child at the same time.

The court may also make orders under s 8 or s 16 CA 1989 (Family
Assistance) orders of its own volition, if necessary.

In *Birmingham CC v H* [1994] 1 All ER 12; [1994] 1 FLR 224, the court
held that in a Pt IV application concerning a child whose parent was
herself still a minor, the welfare of the child subject to the application
was paramount.

2.2 Delay is deemed prejudicial to child's interests (and the impact of the new Public Law Outline)

In any proceedings in which any question with respect to the upbringing
of a child arises, the court shall have regard to the general principle

that any delay in determining the question is likely to prejudice the welfare of the child (s 1(2) of the Children Act).

The courts have been greatly concerned about delays in the family court system. The first attempt at grasping the nettle was an interim *Protocol for Judicial Case Management* issued in 2003. This is now replaced by the *Public Law Outline* (PLO), issued as *Practice Direction: Guide to Case Management in Public Law Proceedings* by the President of the Family Division, and operative from 1 April 2008. It is available at www. justice.gov.uk/guidance/careproceedings.htm.

Under the PLO, the cases progress through four stages:

(1) Pre issue process up until the end of the first hearing;
(2) The Advocates Meeting and the Case Management Stage;
(3) Issues Resolution Hearing and the preceding Advocates Meeting;
(4) Final Hearing and Directions for disclosure at the conclusion of the case.

The court regulates the conduct of cases by use of questionnaires, pro formas, meetings, hearings and directions. In these, the court establishes who are parties to, or who should have notice of, the proceedings. The court ensures that the evidence is in order and service is carried out. A timetable is set for preparation of the case and disclosure of evidence to other parties and the children's guardian, and a hearing date fixed. Directions given carry the force of court orders, failure to comply with them will be viewed by the court seriously and a full explanation for non-compliance will be required. Sanctions include wasted costs orders against those parties to a case who cause (or negligently allow) unnecessary delay. See *Ridelhalgh v Horsfield and Watson v Watson* [1994] 3 WLR 462; [1994] 3 All ER 848; [1994] 2 FLR 194 for the Court of Appeal's guidance on wasted costs.

2.3 No order unless necessary in the interests of the child

The Act assumes that the parties will do their best to resolve differences by negotiation and co-operation. Section 1(5) of the Children Act 1989 provides that the court has a positive duty not to make an order unless it is in the interests of the child to do so. This is referred to as the 'non-intervention' principle. See *Re W* [1994] 2 FCR 1216, in which the Court of Appeal discussed this principle in an application for a contact order.

3 Parental Responsibility

On 19 October 1991, ss 2 and 3 of the Children Act 1989 changed the status of parents in relation to their children, by creating the concept of 'parental responsibility'.

Amazingly, many parents are unaware of these changes, and they are also unaware that not all parents have parental responsibility for their children. Parental responsibility may be shared with others and it may be delegated in part, but it may not be surrendered or transferred entirely save by adoption. Each person who has parental responsibility may exercise it without a duty to consult others who also have it, with certain exceptions, but in the event of disagreement or a need for child protection, its exercise is also subject to orders of the court. People who have a Special Guardianship Order in their favour may exercise their parental responsibility in priority over others.

3.1 Definition, powers and duties of parental responsibility

Section 3(1) of the Children Act defines parental responsibility as:

> All the rights, duties, powers, responsibilities and authority which by law a parent of a child has in relation to the child and his property.

This wonderfully vague definition is not clarified anywhere in the Children Act except in s 3(2), which states that parental responsibility includes the powers of a guardian in looking after a child's property, for example, to give a valid receipt for a legacy. Paragraph 1.4 of the *Introduction to the Children Act 1989* (1991) says: 'That choice of words emphasises that the duty to care for the child and to raise him to moral, physical, and emotional health is the fundamental task of parenthood and the only justification for the authority it confers.'

The Children Act 1989 Regulations and Guidance Vol 1 *Court Orders*, (2008) para 2.6, says that parental responsibility is concerned with bringing the child up, caring for him and making decisions about him, but does not affect the relationship of parent and child for other purposes. It does not affect rights of maintenance or succession.

Some statutory powers are reliant upon parental responsibility:

(a) appointment of guardian for a child in the event of death (Children Act, s 5(3));

(b)   consent to the adoption of the child (Adoption Act 1976, s 16);

(c)   access to the child's medical records (Access to Health Records Act 1990, ss 4, 5 and 12);

(d)   consent to a child's marriage (Marriage Act 1941, s 1 as amended by Sch 12, para 5 of the Children Act);

(e)   consent of all those with parental responsibility or leave of the court is required for removal of a child from the country, failing which a criminal offence is committed (Child Abduction and Custody Act 1985, s 1).

This provision applies even if there is a residence order in force, but under s 13(2) of the Children Act, the person holding a residence order in his or her favour may take the child abroad for holiday purposes for up to one month. The court may, of course, grant additional or general leave to take the child abroad for longer periods or permanently.

Other decisions and powers of those with parental responsibility include:

(a)   Consent to medical assessment, examination or treatment. See below, 3.1.2 and Chapter 12.

'Nearest relative' in the Mental Health Act 1983, s 27(2) is now amended to substitute for the word 'mother' both the mother and the father who has parental responsibility within the meaning of s 3 of the Children Act.

(b)   Lawful correction. It is a defence to assault or to a charge of ill treating a child under s 1 Children and Young Persons Act 1933 for a parent to prove that the act was one of 'lawful correction'. The correction must be 'moderate in manner, instrument and quantity.' See *R v H (Assault of Child: reasonable Chastisement)* [2001] EWCA Crim 1024 [2001] 2 FLR 431.

(c)   Application for or veto of child's passport. *Practice Direction* [1986] 1 All ER 977, p 981 and *Re A* [1995] 1 FLR 767.

(d)   Right to represent child as 'next friend' in all court proceedings where the child is a party except cases involving child protection or the upbringing of the child. The right can be removed if the parents act improperly or against the interests of the child (RSC Ord 80 r 2, CCR Ord 10 r 1).

(e)   Right to name or re-name child. If both parents have parental responsibility and they agree, there is no problem. Please note *Practice Direction* [1995] 1FLR 458 and *Re PC (Change of Surname)* [1997] 2 FLR 730 for guidance. In cases where one parent wishes to change a child's name, the consent of all others with parental responsibility, or in the absence of consent, the leave of the court is required.

See, also, the Enrolment of Deeds (Change of Name) Regulations 1984 SI 1984/604.

(f) Under the Births and Deaths Registration Act 1953, a baby's name must be registered within 42 days of birth. Parents with parental responsibility may register the name. Fathers without parental responsibility, therefore, have no power to choose or register the baby's name without an order of the court. See *Re PK Re A, and Re B (Change of Name)* [1999] 2 FLR 930 and the House of Lords in *Dawson v Wearmouth* [1999] 1 FLR 1167; [1999] 2 WLR 960, BUT note joint registration of birth at 3.4.3 on page 23.

(g) Right to decide child's education and duty to send their child to school, or to provide suitable alternative schooling, Education Acts 1962 and 1944. Sch 13, para 10 to the Children Act includes those who are not parents but who have parental responsibility for the child. See *Re Z (Minor) (Freedom of Publication)* [1996] 2 WLR 107; [1996] 1 FLR 191 on education, medical consent and publication of information.

(h) Decisions about a child's religion. The courts will not interfere unless the welfare of the child is threatened.

3.1.1 Duration

Parental responsibility lasts until a child is 18 years old if it belongs to the mother; child's married father; father with a parental responsibility agreement, legitimation, joint registration; or other person with a court order. Parental responsibility can be ordered with residence orders or guardianship. See below, 3.4.4. and 3.5.4.

3.1.2 Parental responsibility and medical consent

Save in emergencies, no person may be given medical treatment without consent. Whatever the motivation, this may constitute an assault for which practitioners may incur liability in tort or criminal law. Detention in hospital or any other place without consent could constitute false imprisonment. Those with parental responsibility, or a court, may give consent for medical assessment or treatment of a child. In emergencies, where there is no person capable or available to give or withhold consent, the doctor may lawfully treat the patient.

Medical records should note who has parental responsibility for a child. With unmarried parents, in the absence of a parental responsibility agreement, joint registration, or court order, only the mother will have parental responsibility for the child. Should she (or any lone person with parental responsibility) die there will be no one with parental responsibility for the child. Single parents should therefore appoint a guardian for their child; see below, 3.4.4.

Young people aged 16 and over

Section 8 of the Family Law Reform Act 1969 confers on a person of 16 the right to give informed consent to surgical, medical, or dental treatment. Examinations or assessments could also impliedly be included. Those who suffer mental illness, disability, or psychiatric disturbance will be subject to the same mental health provisions and safeguards as adults.

Children aged under 16

See below, 12.1 and 12.2.

In *Gillick v West Norfolk and Wisbech AHA* [1986] AC 112, Mrs Gillick challenged her local health authority's provision of contraceptive advice to her daughters under 16 without her consent. The House of Lords supported the health authority's actions. In giving judgment, it formulated the concept known colloquially as '*Gillick* competence'. A child under 16 may make medical decisions according to her chronological age, in conjunction with mental and emotional maturity, intelligence, her comprehension of the nature and consequences of the decision to be made and the quality of the information provided.

The rationale of the *Gillick* case has recently been considered and approved more recently in *R (Axon) v Secretary of State for Health* [2006] EWHC 37 (Admin) QBD, in which abortion for a child under 16 was the subject of the court's consideration. Although distinctions could be made between the issues in *Gillick*, i.e. advice and treatment for contraception and sexually transmitted illnesses on the one hand and abortion in the *Axon* case on the other, which gave rise to more serious and complex issues, the guidelines set out in *Gillick*, properly adapted, were considered appropriate as guidance in respect of all sexual matters. That was because the majority in *Gillick* did not indicate that their conclusions were dependent on the nature of the treatment proposed. The *Gillick* guidelines are of general application to all forms of medial advice and treatment.

In the case of *Re R (Minor: Consent to Medical Treatment)* [1992] Fam 11; [1992] 1 FLR 190, the Court of Appeal held that a '*Gillick* competent' child acquires a right to make decisions equal to that of each of his parents and only the absence of consent by all having that power would create a veto. If they cannot agree, then the doctor lawfully may act on consent of one. However, *A Guide to Consent for Examination or Treatment*, produced by the National Health Service Management Executive, advises that the refusal of an adult or '*Gillick* competent' young person should be respected.

If there is disagreement or refusal concerning medical treatment for a child when a doctor considers it medically necessary, and negotiation fails, then the matter can be resolved under s 8 of the Children Act by a specific issue order. The High Court in its inherent jurisdiction or under the Children Act can override the wishes of anyone in relation to the medical treatment of a child if this is adjudged to be in the child's best interests.

3.1.3 What if there is no one with parental responsibility?

Where immediate action is needed for the welfare of the child and no one with parental responsibility is available, s 3(5) of the Children Act provides that:

A person who:

(a) does not have parental responsibility for a particular child; but

(b) has care of the child, may ... do what is reasonable in all the circumstances of the case for the purpose of safeguarding or promoting the child's welfare.

This could apply to childminders, foster carers, neighbours and others looking after children who may need to take a child quickly to the GP or dentist, etc. This section, however, is not intended to cover consent for major medical issues.

3.2 Legal position of child's birth mother

Parental responsibility always belongs to a mother in relation to the children to whom she has given birth. It does not matter whether she is married to the father of the child (or to anyone else) or not. Nothing can remove that parental responsibility from her save death or adoption of the child. For surrogacy arrangements, see below at sections 3.5.6 and 3.5.7.

3.3 Legal position of child's father

3.3.1 Married fathers

Under s 2(1) of the Children Act, a father automatically has parental responsibility for his child if he was married to the child's mother at the time of the child's birth. This concept includes marriage at the time of the child's conception. See *Re Overbury (Deceased)* [1954] 3 All ER 308. The man must be the biological father. Section 1(2)-(4) of the Family Law Reform Act 1987 includes in the meaning of s 2(1) children who are legitimated by statute. This enables a child's father to gain parental responsibility if he subsequently marries the child's mother after conception or the birth of the child.

We are told by clients that many married couple's arguments have ended with '… and anyway she is not your child!' The parents of a legitimate child have parental responsibility for that child. The test of legitimacy is that the child is born to parents who are married to each other at the time of the child's birth. The Family Law Reform Act 1987 s 1(2) and 1(3) includes children who are legitimated by their parents' subsequent marriage. A child's legitimacy may be rebutted by cogent evidence, for example, a DNA paternity test showing that the husband is not the father of the child. A married man has no parental responsibility for children who are not biologically his own, even if they are born during the marriage.

Children born to a married couple as a result of artificial insemination will, however, be regarded as the child of the husband provided that the conditions set out in the Human Fertilisation and Embryology Act 1990 are met.

Note that men who become step-parents on marriage do not automatically acquire parental responsibility for their spouses' children, see below, 3.5.2.

3.3.2 Unmarried fathers

A father who is not married to the mother of his child has no parental responsibility, but he can acquire it in a number of ways. These are set out below.

3.4 Acquisition and loss of parental responsibility by child's birth father

3.4.1 Parental responsibility order

A father may apply under s 4(1)(a) of the Children Act for a Parental Responsibility Order.

Applicant

The father (no one else can apply).

Parties/respondents

All those with parental responsibility (or if a care order is in force, those who had parental responsibility immediately prior to that order). On discharge application, all parties to the original proceedings. FPC(CA)R 1991 Sch 2 col (iii) and FPR 1991 App 3 col (ii).

Notice

Local authority providing accommodation for the child. Person(s) with whom the child is living at time of application, FPC(CA)R 1991 Sch 2 col (iv) and FPR 1991 App 3 col (iv). Person providing certified refuge for the child (see s 51 of the Children Act).

Status of child

With leave, a child of sufficient age and understanding can oppose the application or apply to set aside the order.

Procedural notes

Family proceedings under Children Act. Application on form C1 or C2 FPC(CA)R 1991 Sch 1 and FPR 1991 App 1. Service at least 14 days before date of directions/hearing. Respondents – copy application, date and time of directions/hearing. Notice – notification of application also date and time of hearing. The remaining procedure is the same as for s 8 applications, see below, Chapter 13.

Attendance

All parties shall attend, unless otherwise directed. The rules make an exception that proceedings shall take place in the absence of any party (including the child) if he is represented by children's guardian or solicitor, and it is in the child's interests having regard to the issues or evidence (FPC(CA)R 1991 r 16(2) and FPR 1991 r 4.16(2)).

Issues for the court

Degree of attachment between father and child; commitment shown by father to child; the reasons for the application (not improper or wrong). Children Act principles – welfare of child paramount; no delay; no order unless it is in best interests of child to make it.

Relevant cases: *Re G (Minor) (Parental Responsibility Order)* [1994] 1 FLR 504; *Re T (Minor) (Parental Responsibility)* [1993] 2 FLR 450; *Re S (Parental Responsibility)* [1995] 2 FLR 648; *Re M (Contact: Family Assistance: McKenzie Friend)* [1999] 1 FLR 75; and *Re J (Parental Responsibility)* [1999] 1 FLR 784.

3.4.2 Parental responsibility agreement with the mother

The mother and father may agree that the father shall have parental responsibility for the child. The agreement must be made in accordance with the Children (Parental Responsibility Agreement) Regulations 1991, SI 1991/1478 as amended by the Parental Responsibility Agreement (Amendment) Regulations 1994 SI 1994/3157 and the Parental Responsibility Agreement (Amendment) Regulations 2005 SI 2005/2808.

The prescribed form C (PRA1) for use by the mother of the child and the father, is straightforward, and must be completed, signed by the mother and father and witnessed by a Justice of the Peace, justices' clerk, or a court officer. The child's birth certificate should be produced, together with proof of identity incorporating a signature and photograph, for example a photocard driving licence, official pass, or passport.

Note that, under s 4A CA 1989, a step-parent who is the married partner or (following the implementation of the Civil Partnership Act 2004) who is the civil partner of a parent with parental responsibility for a child may enter into a parental responsibility agreement with the parent(s) of the child. In this case, the parental responsibility agreement will be on form C (PRA2) and the same proofs if identity will be required. In addition, proof of the marriage or civil registration will be necessary. The completed and witnessed form C (PRA2) then has to be registered with the Principal Registry of the Family Division, at First Avenue House, 42-49 High Holborn, London, WC1V 6NP, and will take effect once it is registered. A copy is sent to each parent.

The precedents for both forms are set out in the Schedule to the Parental Responsibility Agreement (Amendment) Regulations 2005 SI 2005/2808. They can be found at website: http://www.opsi.gov.uk/si/si200528.htm

3.4.3 Joint Registration of the birth by father and mother

This was a new provision brought in by the Adoption and Children Act 2002 and it applies only to registrations of birth made on or after 1 December 2003. It is possible to re-register the birth of a child born before this date, where the original registration did not name the father, provided that the requirements of the Births and Deaths registration Act 1953, s 10(a) are met. In these circumstances, the parental responsibility will run from the date of registration and not from the date of birth. The mother must agree to the inclusion of the father at the registration of the birth. Registration can unilaterally be applied for where there is a court order in force for parental responsibility or financial relief, or a parental responsibility agreement is in force.

3.4.4 Residence order and parental responsibility

A child's father may acquire a residence order under s 8 of the Children Act. This may be granted on application or of the court's own volition in the course of family proceedings, see below, Chapter 13.

The court has power to award parental responsibility with residence orders which subsists while the order remains in force. Residence orders expire by effluxion of time when the child reaches 16, unless there are exceptional circumstances, in which case it can be extended to age 18.

However, there are special provisions in the Children Act when the father of a child acquires a residence order relating to his child. On making the residence order, the court must also grant parental responsibility to the father, under ss 4 and 12(1) of the Children Act. The court shall not bring that parental responsibility order to an end whilst the residence order remains in force. The parental responsibility so granted will not expire with the residence order (for example, when the child reaches 16) but will last until the child is 18, unless the court specifically brings the father's parental responsibility to an end earlier, s 91(7) of the Children Act.

In specific circumstances, the father of a child who does not have parental responsibility may also acquire it (in the same way as another relative or non-relative might), through one or more of the ways outlined in section 3.5. below, where an application is open to him, for example, where appropriate, he may apply for guardianship.

3.5 Acquisition of parental responsibility by others

3.5.1 Relatives

Relatives can obtain parental responsibility for a child along with a residence order under ss 8 and 12(2) CA 1989. Relatives could also seek an appointment under s 5 CA 1989 as guardian of the child, which automatically gives them parental responsibility until the child reaches 18 or the court orders otherwise, s 91(7) CA 1989.

A relative could also, in theory, apply to adopt a child in order to gain parental responsibility. Courts will not usually favour adoption by relatives because the effect of adoption is to sever all legal ties with existing parents and therefore may complicate family relationships, but in specific circumstances it may be considered appropriate.

In referring to relatives, it is important to note that, in relation to applications under the CA 1989, civil partners are treated in law in the same way as a married spouse. For example, a civil partner of a parent with parental responsibility can enter into a parental responsibility agreement with that child's parent(s), subject to certain conditions, see section 3.4. above.

3.5.2 Step-parents

Step-parents do not acquire parental responsibility for the children of their partners automatically on marriage. Currently, they can only acquire parental responsibility along with a residence order under ss 8 and 12(2) CA 1989, or by adoption.

The courts would not normally favour adoption by a step-father unless the natural father is deceased, whether the natural father had parental responsibility or not, since adoption would sever his legal responsibility for, and relationship with, his child.

A step-parent who is married to a parent with parental responsibility of the child or who is the civil partner of that parent, can acquire parental responsibility for the child by entering into a parental responsibility agreement with the parent(s) of the child under s 4 CA 1989, for details of how to do this, see section 3.4.2 above.

The mother of a child (who always has parental responsibility herself) may develop terminal illness or die whilst in a relationship with a man who is not the father of her child. The child may be very attached to him and he may be committed to the care of the child.

If the child's mother dies, there are three possible scenarios:

(a) The child's biological father is alive but has no parental responsibility. The child will then legally have no one with parental responsibility.

Remedies:

- before the mother's death, the stepfather obtains a residence order alone or shared with the mother;
- mother appoints the stepfather guardian under s 5;
- if the mother has died, the stepfather may obtain a residence order or guardianship order under s 5(1)(a). Guardianship automatically gives him parental responsibility until the child reaches 18 or the court orders otherwise, s 91(7)

The step-parent may apply for a special guardianship order under s 14A CA 1989 which will enable him to have parental responsibility for the child and create stronger legal ties with the child, but this is less final than adoption, which would sever legal links with the child's birth family. Under a special guardianship order, links with the child's birth family are retained.

(b) If the child's biological father is alive and has parental responsibility.

The biological father will then automatically hold the legal responsibility for the child.

The stepfather can seek a residence order. If he has been appointed as guardian by the mother before her death, this will only be effective immediately if she had a residence order in her favour before her death, s 5 (7) (b) of the Children Act. He could seek guardianship under s 5(1)(b) if the deceased mother had a residence order in her favour. In either case, he would have to share parental responsibility with the biological father and resolve disputes by seeking an appropriate s 8 order. See below, Chapter 15 for discussion of s 8 orders.

The stepfather can enter into a parental responsibility agreement with the father who has parental responsibility, under s 4 CA 1989 (see 3.4.2. above)

(c) If the biological father is dead, then there is no one with parental responsibility for this child.

The stepfather can seek a residence order under s 8 or guardianship under s 5(1)(a) of the Children Act. Guardianship automatically gives him parental responsibility until the child reaches 18 or the court orders otherwise, s 91(7).

The stepmother of a child, living with the child's father, would face similar problems on his death. The child's mother would always have parental responsibility. She would have a legal right to the care of the child unless otherwise agreed or ordered by the court. The stepmother could seek a residence order or guardianship, if the father had a residence order in force in his favour at the time of his death.

3.5.3 Non-relatives

Non-relatives may acquire parental responsibility with a residence order or through guardianship, special guardianship, or adoption.

A local authority obtains parental responsibility for a child under s 31 of the Children Act 1989 when a care order is made, sharing parental responsibility with the child's mother and anyone else who has it. The exercise by others of their parental responsibility in relation to the child may be limited by the local authority under the care order, but there should be partnership and co-operation. The local authority does not acquire parental responsibility when looking after children in voluntary arrangements.

3.5.4 Guardianship

The court may appoint a guardian for a child under s 5 of the Children Act where:

- there is no person with parental responsibility for the child; or
- a residence order has been made in favour of a parent or guardian who died whilst the order was in force.

This parental responsibility subsists until the child reaches 18, unless ended earlier by the court, s 91(7).

A parent with parental responsibility, or a guardian, may appoint a guardian for a child in the event of his death under s 5(3) and (4) of the Children Act respectively. If when he dies there is no one else alive with parental responsibility, the appointed guardian will act. If there is anyone with parental responsibility still alive, then the guardian will only be able to act after the death of all others with parental responsibility. If, however, someone with a residence order in her favour appoints a guardian, she will act on the death of the appointer, in conjunction with anyone else remaining alive who has parental responsibility

3.5.5 Special Guardianship Order

Special Guardianship is a new order created by the Adoption and Children Act 2002 and imported into the Children Act 1989 as s 14A. The court can make this order in public or private law proceedings and under the Adoption and Children Act.

The effect of a special guardianship order is that:

*   the special guardian has parental responsibility for the child until the child reaches 18;
*   special guardians can exercise their parental responsibility to the exclusion of others who have it.

The order is available to non-parents and non-relatives. The child's parents are specifically excluded from application.

Applications may be made by people including:

*   guardians;
*   people with a residence order in their favour;
*   a person with whom the child has lived for three years;
*   a person who has the consent of the local authority in respect of a child in their care;
*   any person with the consent of all those who have parental responsibility for the child;
*   any person with leave of the court (CA 1989 ss 10(8) and (9) apply.

The court can make this order of its own motion in family proceedings.

Local authorities must make special guardianship services available (including counselling, mediation, and resources which may include cash assistance) under s 14F CA 1989 and the Special Guardianship Regulations 2005 reg 3.

For the distinction between the effects of special guardianship and a residence order, see *Birmingham City Council v R* [2006] EWCA Civ 1748, 1FLR 564, and for a contrast with adoption, see *Re S (Adoption Order or Special Guardianship Order)* [2007] EWCA Civ 54, 1FLR 819.

The order can be discharged on the application of the birth parents, but is not to be discharged unless there is a significant change of circumstances since the order was made.

3.5.6 Parental responsibility, surrogacy, and the Human Fertilisation and Embryology Act 1990

Where a surrogate mother is the genetic mother, she is the child's legal mother and has parental responsibility for the child born to her, s 2 (1) CA 1989. The same legal status applies when the surrogate mother was artificially impregnated with an embryo or with eggs, under the provisions of s 27 of the Human Fertilisation and Embryology Act 1990 (HFEA). Before the coming into force of the HFEA on 1 August 1991, the FLRA 1987 made similar provisions.

The married husband of the surrogate mother, if he consented to the artificial insemination, also has parental responsibility under s 28 HFEA.

If he did not consent, then he has no parental responsibility for the child, and has step-parent status.

3.5.7 Parental Orders under s 30 of the Human Fertilisation and Embryology Act 1990

The HFEA allows a married couple who have agreed with a surrogate mother to commission the birth of a child to apply under s 30 for a Parental Order that they be treated in law as the parents of that child.

The conditions on the making of a Parental Order include that:

- the applicants are over 18;
- the application was made within six months of the birth of the child;
- the birth mother was a surrogate mother and that she and the father (if has parental responsibility for the child – see 3.4.5 above) agree to the making of the order. The agreement is to be given after six weeks from the child's birth. The court can dispense with agreement in specified circumstances, see s 30(5);
- the child was living with the applicants at the time of the application;
- no money or benefit has been handed over save for reasonable expenses incurred.

4 *Every Child Matters*: Child Protection Procedures in Health and Social Work

Current child protection procedures are formed to operate within the framework of the Children Act 1989 (CA 1989) and the Children Act 2004 (CA 2004), underpinning the *Every Child Matters: Change for Children* Programme which includes the provisions for the establishment of Local Safeguarding Children Boards.

The child protection procedures are set out in a number of publications. They are all accessible at: www.everychildmatters.gov.uk.

The main publication is *Working Together to Safeguard Children* (2006) referred to below as *Working Together*. This forms part of a suite of five documents which underpin *Every Child Matters* and are:

- *Inter-Agency Co-operation to Improve Wellbeing of Children: Children's Trusts* describes the duties placed on local authorities and other key partners to co-operate to improve the wellbeing of children and young people.

- *Duty to Make arrangements to Safeguard and Promote the Welfare of Children* sets out the key arrangements agencies should make to safeguard and promote the welfare of children in the course of discharging their normal functions.

- *Children and Young People's Plan* supports the fulfilment of both the co-operation and safeguarding and promoting welfare duties.

- *The Role and Responsibilities of the Director of Children's Services and the Lead Member for Children's Services*

- The chapter on Local Safeguarding Children's Boards within the revised version of *Working Together*

The Children Act 1989 is clarified and explained by the volumes of *Guidance and Regulations*, listed above, at 1.5. These volumes of guidance and Part 1 of *Working Together* are all mandatory guidelines issued under s 7 of the Local Authority Social Services Act 1970.

Local authorities must follow that guidance, unless local circumstances indicate exceptional reasons that justify a variation, and any departure from it must be justified in respect of any complaints procedure or judicial review.

Chapters 3, 4, 7 and 8 of *Working Together* are also issued under s 16 of the Children Act 2004, which states that Children's Services Authorities and each of the statutory partners must, in exercising their functions relating to a Local Safeguarding Children Board (LSCB), have regard to any guidance given to them for the purpose by the Secretary of State. This means that they must take the guidance into account and, if they decide to depart from it, have clear reasons for doing so.

Other key policy and planning documents relating to *Every Child Matters* include:

*   *The National Service Framework for Children, Young People and Maternity Services*, which sets out a 10-year programme to stimulate long-term and sustained improvement in children's health and wellbeing.

*   *Every Child Matters: Change for Children – Young People and Drugs*, which gives guidance on co-operation and joint planning to counter drug misuse.

*   *Duty on Local Authorities to Promote the Educational Achievement of Looked After Children*, which sets out the implications of the new duty in the Children Act 2004 for local authorities, strategic planning, joint area reviews and day-to-day working practices.

*   *The Framework for the Inspection of Children's Services*, which sets out the principles to be applied by an inspectorate or commission assessing any children's service, and defines the key judgements which, where appropriate and practical, inspections will seek to make. It is available from:www.ofsted.gov.uk.

*   *Sharing Information: Practitioner's Guide* and the supporting materials, which are for everyone who works with children and young people, and explain when and how information can be shared legally and professionally.

Each local authority, district council, NHS body and the police, probation and prison services along with Secure Offending Services, Connexions and Youth Offending Teams have a duty under s 11 CA 2004 to discharge their functions with regard to the need to safeguard and promote the welfare of children. See *Making Arrangements to Safeguard and Promote the Welfare of Children*, published by DfES in August 2005 (www.everychildmatters.gov.uk/resources-andpractice/IG00042/).

Chapter 3 of *Working Together* covers the role of the Local Safeguarding Children Boards (LSCB) in detail. See also The Local Safeguarding Children Boards Regulations 2006, SI 2006/90.

LSCBs are multi-disciplinary groups comprising senior representatives from local organisations and agencies involved in the *Every Child Matters* programme. Each LSCB should develop local policies and procedures, and ensure co-ordination and co-operation between agencies in the implementation of child protection procedures in its locality. Each organisation and agency retains its own line of accountability for operational work. Practitioners should be aware of the policies and procedures developed by the local LSCB in the area in which they work.

4.1 Hierarchy within social services departments

Each social services department will use terminology that is likely to vary geographically. The head of social services may be called the *Director of Social Services*, supported by one or more *Assistant Directors*, each of whom usually has an administrative responsibility related either to an area of work, or to a geographical area.

The local authority children's social care department deals with child protection. Social services departments are generally divided into task related divisions, for example, child care, community care, etc. One *Assistant Director* may have the responsibility for child care, which may or may not include adoption.

Out in the field, the front line work may be divided into geographical areas, headed by a person in managerial role, perhaps called the *Divisional Manager* or *District Manager*. The work is usually carried out by social work teams.

4.2 Referral procedures and preliminary investigations

See Chapter 5 of *Working Together* for detailed guidance on referral procedures, and see the flowchart of local authority referral procedures at Figure 1.

The local LSCB should ensure that organisations and agencies have contact lists of addresses and telephone numbers for referral. A member of the public concerned about a child should contact the police, the local authority children's social care or the NSPCC. Police will usually either use their powers under s 46 CA 1989 in an emergency, or refer the matter to social services.

Social services in each area appoint a 'duty officer' to take referrals. The *duty officer* will note the information given, ask further details to establish the name, whereabouts and circumstances of the child, and request information about the person making the referral if appropriate.

Professionals referring concerns to social services are expected to confirm the referral in writing within 48 hours. This is to ensure that referrals are properly recorded, and not missed or, for other reasons, not followed up. The Common Assessment Framework provides a structure for the written referral. *Working Together* recommends that at the end of any discussion or dialogue about a child, the referrer (whether a professional or a member of the public or family) and LA children's social care should be clear about proposed action, timescales and who will be taking it, or that no further action will be taken. The decision should be recorded by LA children's social care and by the referrer (if a professional in another service). LA children's social care should acknowledge a written referral within one working day of receiving it. If the referrer has not received an acknowledgement within three working days, they should contact LA children's social care again.

When responding to referrals from a member of the public rather than another professional, LA children's social care should bear in mind that personal information about referrers, including identifying details, should only be disclosed to third parties (including subject families and other agencies) with the consent of the referrer. In all cases where the police are involved, the decision about when to inform the parents (about referrals from third parties) will have a bearing on the conduct of police investigations.

Where no further action is to be taken by the local authority, feedback should be provided to the referrer, who should be told of this decision and the reasons for making it. We should emphasise here the important role of the Independent Reviewing Officer (IRO) at the end of proceedings. The IRO is appointed by the local authority to regularly review the implementation of the care plan for all children in local authority care, bearing in mind the needs and welfare of the child. In theory at least, the IRO now takes on the independent monitoring and oversight role which was previously fulfilled by the Guardian and solicitor for the child.

A child at risk of significant harm is, by definition, a child in need. In most cases, a child in need would remain at home, helped by the provision of appropriate services, resources and advice for the family. However, some children need greater levels of protection. The local authority must therefore carry out an initial assessment in accordance

Figure 1: Local Authority Referral Procedures

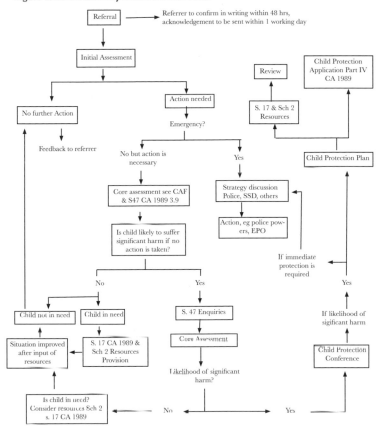

with the *Framework for Assessment of Children In Need and Their Families*, (the *Assessment Framework*) and decide quickly whether it is necessary to seek emergency protection, child assessment or any other Children Act order. See Chapter 16 for details of the assessment process.

The local authority immediately trawls for information from the referrer, police, general practitioner, and others to whom the family is known. This is known as undertaking 'Safeguarding checks'. *Working Together* encourages co-operation with parents in child protection:

Involving of children and families

In the process of finding out what is happening to a child, it is important to listen and develop an understanding of their wishes and feelings. The importance of developing a co-operative working relationship is emphasised, so that parents or caregivers feel respected and informed, they believe agency staff are being open and honest with them and, in turn, they are confident about providing vital information about their child, themselves and their circumstances. The consent of children, young people and their parents or caregivers should be obtained when sharing information, unless to do so would place the child at risk of significant harm. Decisions should also be made with their agreement, whenever possible, unless to do so would place the child at risk of significant harm.

Working Together, p 100

Possible outcomes of an initial assessment are:

(a)   no further action needs to be taken;

(b)   protection can be achieved by working in co-operation with the parents and provision of services, etc;

(c)   s 47 enquiries and core assessment required;

(d)   child protection conference is required;

(e)   urgent court proceedings are necessary.

4.3 Child protection conferences

Child protection conferences bring together the child and their family members with those professionals most involved with them. *Working Together* provides detailed guidance for child protection conferences, reviews and decision making processes in paras 5.80-5.135.

4.3.1   Purpose

The purpose of the child protection conference is to:

*   bring together the family, child and professionals most involved and analyse evidence about the needs of the child and the parents' or carers' capacity to respond to the child's needs;

*   ensure the child's safety and promote the child's health and development in the context of their wider family and environment.

If the child is at continuing risk of significant harm, the conference must decide what future action is required to safeguard and promote the welfare of the child.

4.3.2 Who should be invited to/at a child protection conference?

The parents, carers and child (if of sufficient age and maturity) should be invited. The professionals invited should include all those who can make a significant contribution to the discussion. Those who are invited but cannot attend should be invited to submit a written report.

Invitees should include:

- Child or his/her representative;
- Family members (including wider family where appropriate);
- LA children's social care staff involved with the child and family;
- Foster carers, residential care staff;
- Professionals involved with the child and family (medical, support, education, etc);
- Those involved in investigations (e.g. police);
- Experts if appropriate;
- Legal services;
- Representative of the NSPCC or armed forces where relevant.

4.3.3 Documents

The child protection conference should have before it documents including:

- a LA written report, including any information obtained from the safeguarding checks;
- a chronology of significant events and professional contact with the family;
- information on the capacity of the parents/carers to meet the child's needs and provide protection;
- the expressed views, wishes and feelings of the child, parents and family members;
- an analysis of the implications of the information gained.

The child and parents should be provided with a copy of the LA report before the conference and the contents explained appropriately. They should be helped to think about and convey what they want to say to the conference.

4.3.4 Decisions to be made and actions to be taken

1. Is the child at continuing risk of significant harm?

Test is either:

- the child can be shown to have suffered ill-treatment or impairment of health or development as a result of physical, emotional or sexual abuse or neglect, and professional judgement is that further ill-treatment or impairment are likely; or

- professional judgement, substantiated by the findings of enquiries in this individual case or by research evidence, is that the child is likely to suffer ill-treatment or the impairment of health or development as a result of physical, emotional or sexual abuse; or

- neglect.

2. The child may be a child in need (but not subject to a child protection plan) and a child in need plan can be drawn up and reviewed every six months.

3. If the child is at continuing risk of significant harm, then inter-agency help will be required, delivered through a child protection plan.

4. If a child protection plan is required, then the Child Protection Conference Chair will determine the category (or categories) of abuse, (physical, sexual, emotional or neglect).

5. *The child protection plan.* Must be agreed in detail.

6. The Conference must agree on the appointment of key worker, and establish the core group of professionals and family members who will implement the plan.

7. Agree upon the child protection plan – and upon the responsibilities of the core group members and family.

8. Agreement on provision of resources for child/family by the agencies.

It should be noted that it is not good practice for a child to remain subject to a child protection plan for long periods of time.

The chair is usually employed by social services, but independent, with no line-management responsibility for case work with the family involved. Attendance at child protection conferences is by invitation, which should include all professionals involved with the family, the parents and carers of the child and the child if of sufficient age and understanding. The chair should ensure that invitees are made welcome, and comfortable, with provision of refreshments, lavatories and other necessities. Minutes should be taken, and decisions recorded. Exclusions should be by the conference chair, and only when justified,

Figure 2: Process of Child Protection Conference

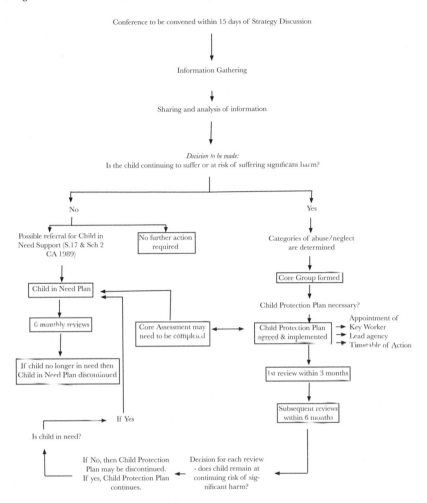

for example, by a strong risk of violence. The chair is usually assisted by a minute taker, and may call upon specialist advice to assist on racial, ethnic, cultural, legal or religious matters, and psychologists or medical specialists where necessary.

The conference should focus on the needs of the child. Parents and older children may bring with them a supportive adult, whose role is to facilitate their comfort and expression of information and concerns to the conference. They may ask questions for clarification via the chair. Solicitors or legal staff may attend to support a child or parents, but not in an adversarial role, see *The Children Act Advisory Committee Handbook of Best Practice in Children Act Cases 1997*, *Representation of Children in Public Law Proceedings* (2006), and the *The SFLA Guide to Good Practice for Solicitors Acting for Children* (2002).

A review of the child protection plan should regularly follow a child protection conference. The first should take place within three months of the conference. The following reviews should take place at no more than six monthly intervals. Extra reviews may be convened at the request of other professionals.

The provision of resources under s 17 and Sch 2 of the Children Act is a statutory duty for a child in need, see, below, 4.6, and should not depend on registration.

4.3.5 Categories of abuse

Neglect

Persistent or severe neglect of a child, failure to protect from danger, extreme failure to carry out aspects of care resulting in impairment of child's health or development, including non-organic failure to thrive.

Physical injury

Actual or likely physical injury to a child, and failure to prevent physical injury or suffering, including deliberate poisoning, suffocation etc and Munchhausen's syndrome by proxy.

Sexual abuse

Actual or likely sexual exploitation of a child or adolescent. The child may be dependent and/or developmentally immature.

Emotional abuse

Actual or likely severe adverse effect upon the emotional or behavioural development of a child caused by persistent or severe emotional ill treatment or rejection. All abuse involves some form of emotional ill treatment. This category should be used where it is the sole or the main form of the abuse.

4.3.6 Criteria for discontinuance of the child protection plan

- No longer a continuing risk of significant harm requiring safeguarding;
- Child and/or family moved permanently to another area;

- Requirement that the new area LA takes over the responsibility for future management of the case within 15 days;

- Child reaches 18, or dies.

4.4 Assessment of risk

See *Working Together to Safeguard Children* (2006); *Framework for the Assessment of Risk* (2000); *Assessing Children in Need and Their Families* (2000); the range of *Initial and Core Assessment Records* for children of different age groups (2000); and the *Family Pack of Questionnaires and Scales* (2000). See, also, below more detailed discussion in Chapter 16.

Local authorities on referral assess the likelihood of significant harm to a child, that is, evaluation of the potential risk to the child should she remain within her family, or the risk to the child if removed from home. After registration there should follow a carefully planned and structured comprehensive assessment within the child protection plan, to gain a better understanding of the child's situation.

Comprehensive assessments require co-operation of agencies and professionals involved with the family. Ask professionals involved about how long they will need, the venue, timing, and personnel to carry out the assessment: all must be clearly agreed.

4.5 Child protection plan

Child protection plans should not be confused with the care plans which are required in care proceedings; see below, Chapters 7 and 16.

Paragraphs 5.116-5.135 of *Working Together* address the formulation and implementation of child protection plans made between family and professionals. Once the plan is agreed, each person should take responsibility to implement their part of it and to communicate with the others involved, with contingency provisions for crises and regular review. Parents and older children should have a copy of the plan, be informed of the nature and purposes of the interventions offered, and confirm that they agree with the plan and are willing to work with it. If the family has particular preferences about the protection work which are not accepted by the professionals, then the professionals' reasons should be explained to the family, together with the right of the family to complain or to make representations.

The child protection plan should:

- Be in writing, in clear language, setting out the expectations and responsibilities of each party;

- Describe the identifiable needs of the child and what therapeutic services are required;

- Include specific, achievable, child-focused outcomes intended to safeguard and promote the welfare of the child;

- Include realistic strategies and specific actions to achieve the planned outcomes;

- Include a contingency plan to be followed if circumstances change significantly and require prompt action;

- Clearly identify roles and responsibilities of professionals and family members, including the nature and frequency of contact by professionals with children and family members;

- Lay down points at which progress will be reviewed, and the means by which progress will be judged; and

- Set out clearly the roles and responsibilities of those professionals with routine contact with the child – e.g. health visitors, GPs and teachers – as well as those professionals providing specialist or targeted support to the child and family.

The plan should be explained, and agreed with the child and the family.

4.6 Child and Family Court Advisory Support Service (CAFCASS)

Following a consultation paper in 1998, the Government made radical changes to the family court advisory system, unifying the Children's Guardian and Reporting Officer Service; the Family Court Welfare Service; and the Children's Branch of the Official Solicitor's Department, to form the Children and Family Court Advisory and Support Service (CAFCASS), with the motto 'children first'.

Information can be obtained from the CAFCASS government website at www.cafcass.gov.uk and at the website for NAGALRO (the organisation for guardians and reporting officers), www.nagalro.com.

CAFCASS's functions are to:

- safeguard and promote the welfare of children who are the subject of family proceedings;

- give advice to any court about any application made to it in such proceedings;

- make provision for children to be represented in such proceedings;

- provide information, advice and other support for children and their families.

The CAFCASS Officer (who might be a CAFCASS employee or a self-employed contractor), is appointed by the court to undertake one or more of their functions, and can be referred to by this general title. CAFCASS Officers have different roles in private and public law proceedings:

- Children's Guardians, who are appointed to safeguard the interests of a child who is the subject of specified proceedings under the Children Act 1989, or who is the subject of adoption proceedings;
- Parental Order Reporters, who are appointed to investigate and report to the court on circumstances relevant under the Human Fertilisation and Embryology Act 1990;
- Children and Family Reporters, who prepare welfare reports for the court in relation to applications under s 8 of the Children Act 1989 (private law proceedings, including applications for residence and contact). Increasingly they also work with families at the stage of their initial application to the court.

CAFCASS Officers can also be appointed to provide support under a Family Assistance Order under the Children Act 1989. (LA officers can also be appointed for this purpose.)

The CAFCASS Officer has a statutory right in public law cases to access and take copies of LA records relating to the child concerned and any application under the Children Act 1989. That power also extends to other records that relate to the child and the wider functions of the LA, or records held by an authorised body (e.g. the NSPCC) that relate to that child.

Where a CAFCASS Officer has been appointed by the court as Children's Guardian and the matter before the court relates to specified proceedings (specified proceedings include public law proceedings; applications for contact; residence, specific issue and prohibited steps orders that have become particularly difficult can also be specified proceedings) they should be invited to all formal planning meetings convened by the LA in respect of the child. This includes statutory reviews of children who are accommodated or looked after, child protection conferences, and relevant Adoption Panel Meetings. The conference chair should ensure that all those attending such meetings, including the child and any family members, understand the role of the CAFCASS Officer.

4.7 Local authority duty to promote welfare of children in their area

Section 17 and Sch 2 to the Children Act 1989 impose on local authorities a duty to promote the welfare of children in their area, with special provision for 'children in need', and children under five years old. Schedule 2 CA 1989 provides a list of the services and resources that may be provided. Local authorities must now implement the recommendations of *Every Child Matters* and comply with the wealth of guidance discussed earlier in the first paragraphs in this chapter.

Local authorities must provide family centres as appropriate for children in its area with counselling advice or guidance, occupational, social or recreational activities, Sch 2, para 9(1) to the Children Act. Local authorities may provide recreational facilities, s 19(1) of the Local Government (Miscellaneous Provisions) Act 1976. Section 18 of the Children Act requires provision of day care for children under school age and for those of school age outside school hours or in the holidays. Section 17(6) of the Children Act authorises financial help in exceptional circumstances.

4.7.1 Duty to investigate potential or actual harm to child

Section 47 of the Children Act requires a local authority, when informed that a child who lives or is found in their area is subject to emergency or police protection, or has reasonable cause to suspect that the child is suffering, or is likely to suffer significant harm, to 'make such enquiries as they consider necessary to enable them to decide whether they should take any action to safeguard or promote the child's welfare'. See *Working Together*, Chapters 3, 5 and 6.

The enquiries are intended to establish whether the authority should make any application to the court or exercise their powers under the Children Act. The authority should consider providing accommodation for a child subject to an emergency protection order if they are not already doing so, s 47(3) (b); and, if the child is in police protection, then the authority should consider applying for an emergency protection order, s 47(3)(c). Enquiries include schooling. Refusal of access to the child or denial of information justifies an application for an emergency protection order. The local authority is under a duty to consider and timetable a review, if no present action is required. If action is necessary then the authority is under a duty to take it, s 47(8).

4.7.2 Local Authority duty to children in need

Section 17(1) of the CA 1989 imposes on local authorities a twofold duty:

(a) to safeguard and promote the welfare of children within their area who are in need; and

(b) ... to promote the upbringing of such children by their families,

by providing a range and level of services appropriate to those children's needs.

Under s 17, those services are free to families on income support or family credit, but otherwise may be subject to means-related contributions.

Section 17(10) defines a child being in need if:

(a) he is unlikely to achieve or maintain, or to have the opportunity of achieving or maintaining, a reasonable standard of health or development without the provision for him of services by the local authority ...;

(b) his health or development is likely to be significantly impaired, or further impaired, without the provision for him of such services; or

(c) he is disabled.

The services can be provided to the child direct, or to the family for the benefit of the child. Local authorities should publish information about the services in their area. Services are listed in Sch 2 to the Children Act.

'Health', 'development' and 'disabled' are all defined in the Children Act. The term 'disabled' was adopted to conform with the wording of the National Assistance Act 1948. Under s 17(6) of the Children Act assistance may be financial in exceptional circumstances, or in kind.

4.7.3 Services for children and their families

Schedule 2, para 8 of the CA 1989 lists services which local authorities should provide for children living with their families:

- advice, guidance and counselling;
- occupational, social, cultural, or recreational activities;
- home help (which may include laundry facilities);
- facilities for, or assistance with, travelling to and from home for the purpose of taking advantage of any other service provided

under this Act or similar service (includes travel for contact purposes); and

• assistance to enable the child concerned and his family to have a holiday.

4.7.4 Duty to children under five

There is power under s 18 CA 1989 to provide day care for children under school age. *The Children Act 1989 Guidance Regulations* Vol 2 *Family Support, Day Care and Educational Provision for Young Children*, is helpful in giving ideas to practitioners about the nature and standards of the provision to be expected. Watch for new developments in day care and child minding issues, for example, policies on smacking.

4.7.5 Compliance with court order to investigate child's circumstances, s 37 of the Children Act 1989

Under s 37 CA 1989, in any 'family proceedings' in which a question arises as to the welfare of any child, if it appears to the court that it may be appropriate for a care or supervision order to be made, the court may order the local authority to investigate the child's circumstances. The local authority then has to consider whether they should apply for a care or supervision order, provide services for the family, or take any other action with respect to the child, s 37(2). If they decide not to seek an order, their reasons must be reported to the court within eight weeks, as must the services provided or to be provided, and any other action taken or proposed with respect to the child, s 37(3) and (4). The local authority may also need to review the situation and set a date for such a review, s 37(6).

4.7.6 'Looked after' children: responsibility of the local authority

Local authorities may provide accommodation for certain children in need, whether voluntarily at the request of the child' parents or carers; under a care order, or for assessment purposes, or otherwise by order of the court, for example where the child is required to live in secure accommodation.

There is strict regulation of the standards of care for children who are accommodated or 'looked after' by local authorities – this includes children who are provided with accommodation by the local authority on a voluntary basis under s 20 CA 1989.

Some children are provided with accommodation under s 59 CA 1989 by voluntary organisations. The local authorities are also responsible for oversight of the standards of this care.

For all 'looked after' children, care plans and regular reviews have to be made under *The Review of Children's Cases (Amendment) Regulations 2004*, and an independent reporting officer (IRO) appointed to oversee the welfare of the child.

5 Emergency Protection Orders

Emergency protection orders are available under s 44 of the Children Act 1989 (CA 1989), as amended by the Family Law Act 1996, s 52, Sch 6, para 3. They are designed for situations when a child needs urgent removal to a safe place; or to be retained in a safe place, such as a hospital. These orders may also be used to obtain access to a child in danger, when urgent action is necessary and/or to exclude a named person from a dwelling house or defined area in which the child lives, and they may include a power of arrest. An order may be made in respect of any child under 18 years of age living or found within the jurisdiction of the court.

5.1 Effects of order

The order gives parental responsibility for the child to the applicant, s 44(5). It authorises the applicant to remove, or retain the child, s 44(4)(b); and operates as a direction to anyone in a position to do so, to produce the child, s 44(4)(a). Under s 44(15) it is a criminal offence to obstruct the applicant in the exercise of his powers under the order.

The order has wide powers, and may contain any or all of these directions:

- authorising doctor, nurse, or health visitor to accompany the applicant to carry out the order, s 45(12) CA 1989;
- for child to have contact with any named person, s 44(6)(a);
- for medical or psychiatric examination of the child, s 44(6)(b);
- requirement to disclose information concerning whereabouts of the child, s 48(1);
- authorisation to enter premises and search for the child, s 48(3);
- authorisation to search for another child in the same premises, s 48(4);
- issue of warrant to police officer to assist the applicant, s 48(9);
- authorisation for nurse, doctor, or health visitor to accompany police, s 48(11);

- exclusion requirement under s 44(A)(2) requiring a named person to leave and remain away from the dwelling house or area in which the child lives;
- undertaking in respect of an exclusion requirement s 44(B); and
- power of arrest in relation to an exclusion requirement s 44(A) (5) and (8).

5.2 Duration

Emergency protection orders last initially for eight days, renewable for a further seven days, s 45(1).

There are some exceptions to this general rule, including the following:

- if the order would expire on public holiday – first order goes to noon on the next day, s 45(2);
- if the child was in police protection (duration 76 hours maximum) before emergency protection order, and the designated police officer is the applicant on behalf of the local authority, the emergency protection order commences from beginning of police protection, s 45(3).

5.3 Grounds for application

The grounds to be proved depend upon who the applicant is.

Since anyone can apply for this order there is a general ground, which is that if the intention is to remove a child to a safe place, the applicant must satisfy the court that there is reasonable cause to believe that the child will suffer significant harm if not removed to accommodation provided by him, and also that there is suitable accommodation available for the child, s 44(1)(A)(i) CA 1989.

If the applicant intends to retain the child in a safe place, then it must be proved that there is reasonable cause to believe that the child is likely to suffer significant harm unless retained in a safe place, s 44 (1)(a)(ii). The grounds can be established on the existence of present harm, or a prognosis indicating a future risk to the child. For the definition of 'significant harm', see below, 7.2 and 7.4.

A local authority applicant has an additional ground. It can satisfy the court that during enquiries made under s 47 CA 1989 about a child in its area, access to the child requested by a person authorised to seek it is being refused unreasonably, and that the access is required as a matter of urgency, s 44(1)(b)(ii) CA 1989. The question of reasonable refusal is a matter for the court. See the *Children Act 1989 Guidance and Regulations* Vol 1 *Court Orders* for examples.

If the application is made by an authorised officer of the local authority, or an 'authorised person' (currently only the NSPCC), there is either the general ground, or an additional ground, that the applicant has reasonable cause to suspect that the child is suffering or is likely to suffer significant harm, that the applicant is making enquiries as to the child's welfare, that access to the child is being unreasonably refused, and access is urgently needed, s 44(1) CA 1989.

The Children Act principles of the paramountcy of the welfare of the child, avoidance of delay and no order unless necessary for the welfare of the child apply. However, the application is not 'family proceedings' within the meaning of s 8(4) CA 1989 and so the 'welfare checklist' does not apply.

5.4 Practice and procedure

5.4.1 Application

Emergency protection orders may be sought by any person. Usually, however, the applicant will be an 'authorised officer' of the local authority, or less commonly, applications may be made by an 'authorised person' (currently only the NSPCC) or 'a designated officer' of the police.

The application should be made in the family proceedings court, unless the local authority has been directed to investigate under s 37, or there are proceedings pending in another court. In these exceptional cases the application can be made in the relevant court, Children (Allocation of Proceedings) Order 1991, Art 3. Application is on form C1, together with form C11. Procedure is governed by *Family Proceedings Courts (Children Act 1989) Rules 1991* (FPC(CA)R 1991) Sch 1 and *Family Proceedings Rules 1991* (FPR 1991) App 1 and r 4.4(4)(a). Applications for extensions should be made to the court which made the original order, Art 4. The application should name the child and, if this is not possible, it should give a description of the child for identification purposes.

A children's guardian will be appointed by the court to oversee the welfare of the child and to advise the court on the child's best interests, see ss 41-42 CA 1989 and below, 15.1.

5.4.2 Respondents

The forms of notice on form C6 plus a copy of the application, with the hearing date endorsed on it, must be served on respondents, together with notice of the date and place of the hearing.

Those listed below are automatically considered respondents to the application:

* everyone with parental responsibility for the child;
* if there is a care order, all those who had parental responsibility immediately prior to the care order;
* the child if of sufficient age and understanding.

See r 7(1), Sch 2 col (iii) FPC(CA)R 1991 and r 4.7(1), App 3 col (iii) FPR 1991. Others may be joined as respondents, and automatic respondents may be removed by direction of the court.

5.4.3 *Ex parte* applications

Application for an emergency protection order may be made *ex parte*, but first, in the family proceedings court, the leave of the justice's clerk or a magistrate must be obtained, r 4(4)(a) FPC(CA)R 1991 and r 4.4(4)(a) FPR 1991.

Applications may be made by telephone to the county court and High Court. The justices clerk may give leave for an *ex parte* application and directions concerning filing in the Family Proceedings Court.

5.4.4 Notice

If an application is made on notice, form C6A, and the date, time and venue of the application must be given within one day of the hearing to:

* parents of the child without parental responsibility;
* any person caring for the child or with whom the child is living when the proceedings are commenced;
* a local authority providing accommodation for the child;
* a person providing a refuge under s 51 CA 1989, in which child lives.

See r 4(1)(b) and Sch 2 col (iv) FPC(CA)R 1991; r 4.4(1)(b) and App 3 col (iv) FPR 1991.

5.4.5 Service

Service must be effected one day before the directions or application hearing, r 4.4(1)(b), Sch 2 FPC(CA)R 1991 and r 4.4.4.(1)(b), App 3 FPR 1991.

5.4.6 Attendance

By r 16(2) FPC(CA)R 1991 and r 4.16.2 FPR 1991, the parties and/or their legal representatives have to attend directions appointments and hearings unless otherwise directed by the court. If respondents fail to appear, the court may proceed in their absence. If applicants fail to attend, the court may refuse their application, rr 16(5) and r 4.16(5).

5.5 Contact, accommodation and the rights of the child

5.5.1 Contact

The child must be allowed reasonable contact with:

- parents;
- those with parental responsibility for the child;
- anyone with whom the child was living before the order;
- anyone with a contact order under s 8 or s 34 in force in respect of the child, or anyone acting on their behalf;
- anyone with an order for access to the child, s 44(13) CA 1989.

The court can control the contact by directions within the emergency protection order. See s 44(13)(dd) and (6)(a) and Sch 14, para 9(4) CA 1989.

The Care of Children, Principles and Practice in Guidance (Principles and Practice), paras 14-16, is relevant to contact issues. See also *Guidance and Regulations* Vol 4 *Residential Care*, paras 2-5-2-6.

5.5.2 Accommodation

The child has the right to accommodation provided, funded or arranged by the local authority and which meets the standards set by *Residential Care*, by the Arrangements for Placement of Children Regulations 1991 and by Sch 2 to CA 1989.

5.5.3 Rights of the child

The child has the right to be returned to his home once the danger has passed and the grounds for the order no longer subsist, s 44(10) CA 1989.

A child of sufficient age and understanding has the right to be consulted and informed about events that are happening, see *Residential Care*, paras 2.20(c), 2.21 and 2.10-2.12.

The emergency protection order may include a direction about medical or psychiatric assessment of the child, s 44 CA 1989. The directions can order or prohibit examinations, either completely or without leave of the court. Directions for examination/assessment can include venue, personnel to be present, and nomination of the person(s) to whom results should be given. A child of sufficient age and understanding has the right to make an informed refusal of medical or psychiatric assessment. A '*Gillick* competent' child, or a young person over 16, may consent to or refuse medical treatment, see Chapter 12 at 12.1 and 12.2.

5.6 Variation and discharge

There is no right of appeal against an emergency protection order, perhaps because of its short duration. It can be challenged by an application to vary or to discharge the order.

The child, child's parents, those with parental responsibility for the child, and anyone with whom the child was living when the order was made, can make an application for variation or discharge, s 45(8) CA 1989.

The rules provide, however, that if a person has had notice of the original application for the emergency protection order, and has attended and opposed the application at the hearing, then there is no right to seek a discharge, s 45(11) CA 1989. There has to be a time lapse of 72 hours after the order is made before there can be a hearing of an application for discharge, s 45(9) CA 1989.

5.7 Exclusion requirement under Emergency Protection Order

The local authority may wish to make arrangements for the removal of an alleged abuser as an alternative to an emergency removal of the child. Under Sch 2 para 5 CA 1989, the local authority has power to assist the alleged abuser in finding alternative accommodation.

Under s 44A(1)-(2) CA 1989, the court can make an exclusion requirement where:

(a) there is reasonable cause to believe that if a person is excluded from the dwelling in which the child lives, the child will cease to suffer or cease to be likely to suffer, significant harm

and

(b) another person living in the dwelling house (whether a parent of the child or some other person):

    (i) is able and willing and able to give to the child the care which it would be reasonable to expect a parent to give him

    and

    (ii) consents to the exclusion requirement.

The consent can be given at court, orally or in writing.

A power of arrest can be attached to the exclusion requirement, under s 44A(5), and if an order is made, then (unless the person to whom it applies was given notice of the hearing and attended the court) it should be announced in open court.

Two notes of caution

• An undertaking from the person required to leave the dwelling house can be accepted instead of an exclusion order, but then no power of arrest can then be attached, s 44B(2).

• If the child is removed from the house to which an exclusion order or undertaking applies for a continuous period of more than 24 hours, the order or undertaking will cease to apply, s 44A(7). If an exclusion order is in force and the child is to be absent from the house for more than 24 hours for any reason which is known in advance, it would be wise to notify the court, and to seek appropriate directions.

6 Child Assessment Orders

6.1 Effects of order

Child assessment orders were created by s 43 CA 1989. It enables the local authority to discover sufficient information about the child to plan appropriate action in the child's interests. *The Children Act 1989 Guidance and Regulations* Vol 1 *Court Orders* suggests that a child assessment order application might usefully follow a s 47 investigation, and that this order might be appropriate ' where the harm to the child is long term and cumulative rather than sudden and severe' (para 4.9.). It is appropriate where there is no evidence of an emergency situation necessitating immediate removal of a child from home for protection, but the parents or carers of the child are demonstrably failing to co-operate with the local authority in facilitating an assessment. The order can stipulate the nature of the assessment sought, the venue and duration, the person(s) to whom the results are to be given, and the contact between the child and others during the subsistence of the order.

6.2 Grounds for application

The court may, by s 43(1) CA 1989, make the order only if it is satisfied that:

- the applicant has reasonable cause to suspect that the child is suffering, or is likely to suffer significant harm;
- an assessment of the child's state of health or development, or of the way in which he is being treated, is required to enable the applicant to determine whether or not the child is suffering or is likely to suffer significant harm; and
- it is unlikely that such an assessment will be made, or be satisfactory, in the absence of an order under this section.

6.3 Practice and procedure

6.3.1 Application

Application can only be made by a local authority or authorised officer (this category currently only includes the NSPCC), see ss 43(1) and (13) and 31(9) CA 1989. It should be on form C1 together with form C16. It must be determined at a full court hearing. Under s 91(15) CA 1989, no further applications may be made without leave in a six month period following disposal of the first application.

6.3.2 Venue

Under the Children (Allocation of Proceedings) Order 1991 SI 1991/1677, the application should be made in the Family Proceedings Court unless there are pending proceedings in another court or the application is the result of a court direction to investigate under s 37 (see above, 4.7.4).

6.3.3 Respondents

Notice plus a copy of the application with the date, time and place of hearing, must be served on those listed below who are automatically regarded as respondents to the application.

These include:

(a)   everyone with parental responsibility for the child;

(b)   the child, if of sufficient age and understanding;

(c)   where there is a care order, everyone with parental responsibility before the making of the care order. See Sch 2 col (iii) of the FPC(CA) 1991 and App 3 col (iii) of the FPR 1991.

Others may be joined as respondents, and automatic respondents may be removed by order of the court, r 7(1) FPC(CA) 1991 and r 4.7(1) FPR. 1991.

6.3.4 Notice

Notice of the proceedings on form C6A and the date, time and venue of the application must be given to those entitled, including:

(a)   parents;

(b)   those with parental responsibility for the child;

(c)   any person caring for the child or with whom the child is living;

(d)   anyone entitled to contact with the child under a contact order under ss 8 or 34 CA 1989 (or former access order);

(e)   a local authority providing accommodation for the child;

(f)   a person providing a refuge in which the child lives under s 51 CA 1989;

(g)   the child, if of sufficient age and understanding.

See r 4(3), Sch 1 and Sch 2 col (iv) FPC(CA)R 1991 and r 4.4(3) and App 3 col (iv) FPR 1991.

6.3.5 Service

Service must be seven days before the directions or application hearing, rule 4.4(1) (b), Sch 2 FPC (CA) 1991 and App 3 FPR 1991.

6.3.6 Generally

The principles in s 1. CA 1989 apply to s 43 applications, save that the welfare checklist does not apply.

Section 8(4)(a) CA 1989 defines 'family proceedings', and within these proceedings the court has power to make other orders of its own volition. Section 43 orders are not 'family proceedings'. This means that the court can only make or refuse the order sought, or treat the application as one for an emergency protection order instead, s 43(3). The court must not make a child assessment order if in all the circumstances of the case the court considers an emergency protection order more appropriate, s 43(4).

The duration of the order is limited to seven days from the date specified for commencement, s 43(5). The Act does not state that the seven days must be consecutive, but there seems no other practicable interpretation. It cannot be extended and, unless the court grants leave, it cannot be renewed until a six month period has elapsed, s 91(15) CA 1989.

6.3.7 Discharge of order

On an application for discharge of a child assessment order, the case will be listed for directions. The procedure is the same as an application for an original order.

6.4 Contact, accommodation and the rights of the child

6.4.1 Contact

There are no specific rules as to contact, but it is submitted that the comments in *The Care of Children, Principles and Practice in Regulations and Guidance*, paras 14-16 and *Guidance and Regulations* Vol 4 *Residential Care* paras 2.5-2.6 relevant to contact with a child in care are applicable to this situation. This would mean that the child should be allowed reasonable contact with:

(a) parents;

(b) those with parental responsibility for the child;

(c) anyone with whom the child was living before the order;

(d) anyone with a contact order under ss 8 or 34 in force in respect of the child, or anyone acting on their behalf;

(e) anyone with an order for access to the child, s 44(13) CA 1989.

The court can control contact by directions within the child assessment order. See s 43(10) CA 1989. Note the operation of Art 8 of the Human Rights Act 1998 (right to family life) as it may affect a child's right to contact with family and siblings.

6.4.2 Accommodation

The child has the right, if removed from home, to reside in accommodation provided, funded or arranged by the local authority which meets the standards set by *Residential Care*, by the Arrangements for Placement of Children Regulations 1991 and by Sch 2 to CA 1989.

6.4.3 Rights of the child

A child of sufficient age and understanding has the right to be consulted and informed about events that are happening; see *Residential Care*, paras 2.20(c), 2.21 and 2.10-2.12.

The child assessment order will usually include a direction about medical or psychiatric assessment of the child. Examinations can be ordered or prohibited. Directions can include venue, personnel to be present, and nomination of the person(s) to whom results of assessments etc should be given. A child of sufficient age and understanding has the right to make an informed refusal of medical or psychiatric assessment, s 43(8) CA 1989. A '*Gillick* competent' child, or a young person over 16, may consent to or refuse medical treatment. See below, Chapter 12.

A child should only be kept away from home where it is absolutely necessary for assessment purposes, and in accordance with directions in the order, s 43(9)(b) and (c) CA 1989.

6.5 Appeals, variation and discharge

Appeal lies against the making or refusal of a child assessment order, from the Family Proceedings Court to the High Court and from the county court or High Court to the Court of Appeal.

Applications to vary or discharge the order may be made on form C1, with two days' notice, to the court which made the original order. See Art 4, Children (Allocation of Proceedings) Order 1991.

Contraventions of the Human Rights Act may be dealt with by complaint, judicial review or appeal against a court order.

7 Care and Supervision Proceedings

In order to avoid too much repetition, all sections and statutory provisions cited below are from the Children Act 1989 (CA 1989) unless otherwise stated.

7.1 Care order - definitions

Care orders are those orders made under s 31 placing a child into the care of a designated local authority. The *designated local authority* is the local authority for the area in which the child resides, or within whose area any circumstances arose in consequence of which the care order is being made.

A *child* is a person under the age of 18, s 105(1). The term *care order* includes an *interim care order* made under s 38 and those orders defined in s 105(1) which have the effect of a care order. Reference to a *child in care*, is defined by s 105(1) to mean a child subject to a care order (and not therefore a child who is 'looked after' by a local authority under a voluntary care arrangement).

7.2 Grounds for application for a care or supervision order

A care order cannot be made in respect of a child over 17 years old, or 16 if married, s 31(3).

Under the CA 1989 there is only one route into statutory care. The court must be satisfied that the criteria set out in s 31 are met and also that an order is necessary for the welfare of the child.

The underlying principles in s 1(1), (2) and (5) – the paramountcy of the welfare of the child, avoidance of delay and no order unless necessary all apply. The court must have regard to the welfare checklist in s 1(3), see Chapter 2 above.

Care orders and supervision orders are mutually exclusive, but the grounds in s 31 for the application for both are the same. On hearing an application for a care order, if the threshold criteria are met, the court may instead order supervision, or vice versa. Where a care order is in force, the court may, at any time during it, substitute supervision, but the making of the supervision order will discharge the existing care order.

Section 31(1) specifies the grounds for application for a care or supervision order:

(a) that the child concerned is suffering, or likely to suffer, significant harm; and

(b) that the harm; or likelihood of harm, is attributable to:

(i) the care given to the child, or likely to be given to him if an order were not made, not being what it would be reasonable to expect a parent to give to him; or

(ii) the child's being beyond parental control.

Definitions from s 31(9), as amended by the Adoption and Children Act 2002:

Harm

Ill treatment or the impairment of health or development, including, for example, impairment suffered from seeing or hearing the ill-treatment of another.

Development

Means physical, intellectual, emotional, social or behavioural development.

Health

Includes physical or mental health.

Ill treatment

Includes sexual abuse and forms of ill treatment which are not physical.

7.3 Significant harm

The difficult part for practitioners in care and supervision proceedings is often the definition and proof of 'significant harm'. Section 31(9) gives the definitions (see above). It is also provided in s 31(10) that: 'Where the question of whether harm suffered by a child is significant turns upon the child's health or development, his health or development shall be compared with that which could reasonably be expected of a similar child.' The court will therefore have to compare this particular child with a notional similar child, of similar background, age, ethnicity, culture, race, religion and physique.

Significant Harm by Adcock, White et al (1991) and *Significant Harm: Its Management and Outcome* by Adcock and White (1998) still provide useful information from a variety of medical and psychological perspectives about the assessment of harm. The reader is led step by step through a logical process of evaluating whether the successive stages of the threshold criteria are met. It helps in case preparation and effective evidence gathering, and assists in explaining the criteria to the court (see Figure 5, p. 111).

Significant harm must be attributable to parental care falling below a reasonable standard, or the child being beyond parental control. The test is objective, measured against a reasonable standard of parenting.

In *Re M (Minor) (Care Order: Threshold Conditions)* [1994] 3 All ER 298 HL; [1994] 2 AC 424; [1994] 3 WLR 558; [1994] 2 FLR 577 the House of Lords held that 'is suffering' means at the date of the hearing, or at the moment when the child protection was initiated, provided that the protection is uninterrupted until the date of the hearing. A careful reading of this judgment is recommended. Whilst the court may find the grounds proved, it may also take account of the circumstances prevailing at the hearing date in considering whether it is necessary to make an order, and which order would be most appropriate.

7.3.1 Standard of proof

The threshold criteria for s 31 proceedings must be established on a 'simple balance of probabilities'. Neither the seriousness of any allegations nor the seriousness of the consequences should make any difference to the standard of proof to be applied in determining the facts. See the recent judgment of the House of Lords in the case of *Re B (Children) (Care orders: Standard ofProof)* (2008) Times Law Reports 12 June 2008. The full impact of the judgment in this case has yet to be seen in subsequent court cases.

'Likely to suffer' refers to a likelihood, and not a balance of probabilities, (i.e. this does not mean a more than 50% chance). The House of Lords put it very clearly as '...a real possibility, a possibility that cannot be sensibly ignored, having regard to the nature and gravity of the feared harm in the particular case ...' See *Re H and others (Child Sexual Abuse: Standard of Proof)* [1996] 1 All ER 1 [1996] 1FLR 80, a s 31 application in respect of four children based on an allegation that the father had sexually abused the oldest child, and positing a likelihood of significant harm to the younger three. The court found that the s 31(2) criteria were not met in the case of the oldest child, leaving no power to go on and even consider the likelihood of harm to the younger three children. These decisions can never be easy to make.

7.4 Practice and procedure

7.4.1 Applicants

Only a local authority or authorised person may apply for a care order, s 31(1). An 'authorised person' at the moment is an officer of the NSPCC, s 31(9).

The court has no power to make a care order without an application, but under s 38(1) it may make an interim care or supervision order on adjourning an application for a full order; or alongside making a direction to the local authority to investigate the child's circumstances under s 37.

7.4.2 Venue

Applications should be made in the Family Proceedings Court, unless one of three exceptions apply: there has been a court directed investigation under s 37 CA 1989; there are pending proceedings; or the application is to extend, vary or discharge an existing order. In these exceptional cases, the application may be made in the same court as the other proceedings, Children (Allocation of Proceedings) Order 1991, Art 3.

County courts are divided into divorce centres, care centres and family hearing centres. Care and supervision applications must be heard in care centres. Refer to the *Family Proceedings (Allocation to Judiciary) Directions 1993* [1993] 2 FLR 1008.

It may be appropriate for a care or supervision application to be heard in a higher court. Transfers are governed by the Children (Allocation of Proceedings) Order 1991 SI 1991/1677; and the Children (Allocation of Proceedings, Appeals) Order 1991 SI 1991/1801 and the Family Proceedings (Amendment) Rules 1991 SI 1991/2113; also, Home Office Circular 45/91. Here there is space only to summarise these provisions, and to draw attention to potential pitfalls which may be encountered. Under Children (Allocation of Proceedings) Order 1991, Art 21, if the procedural requirements are broken, proceedings are not invalidated nor is it ground for appeal.

Certain cases should be heard in the High Court: post-adoption contact applications; specific issue on medical matters; HIV test for a child; injunctions concerning publicity; and applications by a child for leave to apply for a s 8 order. See Chapter 14; *Practice Direction* [1993] 1 WLR 313 and 1 All ER 820; and CA 1989 Advisory Committee Transfer Trigger List (below, 14.3).

7.4.3 Form

Application must be made on form C1 (or C2 if made in existing proceedings) with form C13.

7.4.4 Respondents

Notice of proceedings with date and place of hearing, together with a copy of the application endorsed with the date of the hearing or directions, must be served three days before the hearing on those listed below who are automatically considered respondents to the application:

(a)   everyone with parental responsibility for the child;

(b)   the child, if of sufficient age and understanding.

See rr 4 and 7(1) and Sch 2 col (iii) FPC(CA)R 1991 and rr 4.4 and 4.7(1), App 3 col (iii) FPR 1991. Others may be joined as respondents and automatic respondents may be removed by direction of the court.

7.4.5 Notice

Notice on form C6A, with the date, time and venue of the application must be served three days before the hearing on:

(a)   parents without parental responsibility for the child;

(b)   any person caring for the child or with whom the child is living;

(c)   a local authority providing accommodation for the child;

(d)   a person providing a refuge in which child lives under s 51;

(e)   any person who is party to relevant proceedings in respect of the child.

See r 4(3), Sch 1 and Sch 2 col (iv) FPC(CA)R 1991 and r 4.4(3) and App 3 col (iv) FPR 1991.

7.4.6 Service

Service on those entitled to notice, or on respondents, must be three days before the directions or application hearing, r 4.4(1)(b), Sch 2 FPC(CA)R 1991 and App 3 FPR 1991. The court can dispense with the requirements of service *Re X (Care: Notice of Proceedings)* [1996] 1 FLR 186. The welfare principle does not apply in consideration of service since it is not a substantive application.

7.4.7 Attendance

Proceedings may take place in the child's absence if the court considers this in his interests, having regard to the matters to be discussed or the evidence likely to be given, and he is represented by a solicitor, r 16 FPC(CA)R 1991 and r 4.16 FPR 1991.

By the same rule, the other parties and/or their legal representatives have to attend directions appointments and hearings unless otherwise directed by the court. If respondents fail to appear, the court may proceed in their absence. If applicants fail to attend the court may refuse their application, r 16(5) and r 4.16(5). Directions hearings are used by the court to oversee the timing of the case, the filing and service of evidence, and the appointment of parties and the children's guardian. For discussion of case preparation see Chapter 12 below.

7.5 Interim orders

On adjourning a care or supervision application, the court has the power to make an interim order when satisfied that there are reasonable grounds for believing the circumstances justifying a care order exist, s 38(2). An interim order's maximum duration is an initial maximum of eight weeks, followed by extensions of up to four weeks each. Shorter interim orders are possible, s 38(4) and (5).

(a) The initial interim order may be up to eight weeks.

(b) If the initial order is less than eight weeks, then the second interim order must be no more than a total of eight weeks less the duration of the initial interim order (for example, first order five weeks, second order three weeks; or first order two weeks, second six).

(c) Any subsequent orders must be of no more than four weeks' duration.

The Act seeks to avoid delay in dealing with cases. Courts will not permit repeated interim orders.

On making an interim order, directions may require medical or psychiatric examination or assessment of the child, which a child of sufficient understanding may refuse, s 38(6). (See Chapter 12, below, for the rights of children.) Directions may also prevent the abuse of children by repeated examinations, s 38(7). Directions may also govern the time and venue of the examination, who shall be present and to whom the results will be given.

7.6 Effects of care order

7.6.1 Duration

A care order subsists until the child reaches 18, unless brought to an end earlier by the court, s 91(1) and (12).

It will cease on the making of:

(a) an adoption order under the Adoption and Children Act 2002, s 46(2)(b);

(b) a care order will not take effect whilst a placement order made under the Adoption and Children Act 2002, s 29(1) is in force;

(c) a special guardianship order s 91(5)(a);

(d) a residence order, Children Act, s 91(1);

(e) the making of a supervision order in substitution for a care order, Children Act, s 39(4);

(f) a care order will end when a child goes to live in Northern Ireland, the Isle of Man or the Channel Islands, provided the relevant regulations are satisfied, s 101(4);

(g) the making of an order for discharge of care, Children Act, s 39(1);

(h) if the child goes to live in Northern Ireland, the Channel islands or the Isle of Man then the order may cease to be enforceable, but the regulations about this have not yet been made under CA 1989, s101(4).

7.6.2 Parental responsibility and care plans

The local authority acquires parental responsibility under a care order, sharing it with those who already have it. The local authority may, however, limit the exercise of parental responsibility by others whilst the care order subsists, s 33(3). There are limits on the powers of the local authority during a care order. They may not change a child's religion; consent to his adoption; or appoint a guardian for the child, s 33. The parental responsibility which others had when the care order was made still subsists, but it cannot be exercised in a way which conflicts with a court order, s 2(6) and (8). The child's name may not be changed or the child removed from the United Kingdom without written consent of all with parental responsibility or leave of the court, s 33(7). The local authority may remove the child from the jurisdiction of the court for up to one month, and under Sch 2, para 19, the local authority can make arrangements for a child to live abroad, with certain restrictions. For care plans see LAC (99) 29 and

NAFWC 1/2000 in Wales. See the House of Lords decision in *Re S (Minors) (Care Order implementation of care plan) re W (Minors) (Care Order adequacy of care plan)* [2002] UKHL 10, [2002] 1 FLR 815. The local authority must provide a care plan when applying for a care order, CA s 31A(2) and keep it under review. After the care order is made, the court have limited powers to intervene.

7.6.3 Proportionality, kinship care, and local authority accommodation of the child

Hale LJ said that 'The principle has to be that the local authority works to support, and eventually reunite, the family, unless the risks are so high that the child's welfare requires alternative family care.' *Re C and B (Care Order: Future Harm)* [2001] 1FLR 611.

Proportionality is therefore vital. *The Children Act 1989 Guidance and Regulations* Vol 4 *Residential Care ('Residential Care')* and Vol 3 *Family Placements* govern the placements of children in residential and foster care and placements with their immediate family or in the 'kinship care' of wider family and friends.

There is a duty on the local authority to keep children with their birth family if at all possible, consistent with their welfare, and *The Care of Children, Principles and Practice in Regulations and Guidance* (1991) (*'Principles and Practice'*) paras 5, 8, 9 and 10 emphasise the importance of maintaining family links and of the primary duty to try to keep a child in their family by the provision of resources. A care order and removal of a child is seen as the last resort, and in itself 'a risk to be balanced against others', para 8.

If the child needs to live away from home, then under s 33(1), the local authority has a duty to receive the child into its care once the order is made. The child is the responsibility of the local authority, and it must provide for somewhere to live and maintenance for the child, s 23(1) 7.6.4

7.6.4 Contact with a child in care

Paragraphs 2.6 and 6.26 of *Residential Care* assume that contact with its family is in the best interests of a child in care unless proved otherwise. Parents and others in financial or practical difficulty should receive help with travelling to contact sessions, Sch 2, para 16.

Contact with children in care is subject to the control of the court. This is different from contact in private law, and orders available under s 34 are referred to as 'care contact orders'. The Act requires that children

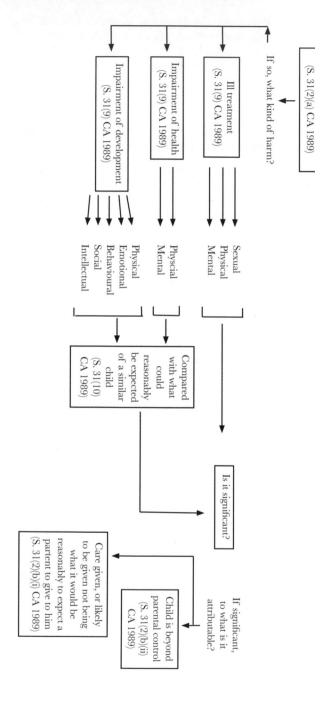

Figure 3: Significant harm flow chart

looked after by a local authority under a care order will be afforded 'reasonable contact' with those people listed in s 34(1). They are:

(a) parents;

(b) guardians;

(c) anyone with a residence order in force immediately before the care order was made;

(d) anyone with care of the child under a High Court order made under its inherent jurisdiction.

The court may, on the application of the Children's Guardian or the child, make whatever order it considers appropriate in respect of contact between the child and any named person. Where the child or the local authority is the applicant, the scope of the order is very wide. On the application of any person entitled to contact under s 34(1) (those listed above), or anyone else with leave of the court, a care contact order may be made.

When the court makes a care order, it may make a care contact order if necessary in the interests of the child, s 34(5). The forms, those entitled to notice and respondents, are the same as for the care order, save that the period of notice is three days, see r 4(1)(b) FPC(CA)R 1991 and r 4.4(1)(b) FPR 1991.

In urgent cases, if necessary, a local authority may stop contact for up to seven days, s 34(6). If it wishes to stop contact for longer, it must apply to the court for a care contact order under s 34, authorising contact with a named person to be curtailed or to be refused. It is argued that severe curtailment of contact is tantamount to a refusal within the meaning of s 34 since the section refers to 'reasonable contact' and the court is the ultimate arbiter of reasonableness.

7.6.5 Rights of the child in care proceedings and under a care order

A child in care has rights which are protected by the Human Rights Act 1998, CA 1989 and also by the guidance issued under it. The child has a right to:

(a) refuse medical or psychiatric assessment ordered within an interim care order under s 38(6) CA 1989;

(b) contact with his or her family (see 7.6.4 above) and *Principles and Practice* paras 9 and 13-16;

(c) consultation on issues involving her care (see *Family Placements*, paras 2.21 and 6.4; also, *Residential Care*, paras 2.21 and 2.45; ss 22(4), 61 and 64 CA 1989; para 25 *Principles and Practice*);

(d)   information about issues involving his care;

(e)   have her wishes and feelings taken into account, ss 22(4), 61 and 64 CA 1989 and para 25 *Principles and Practice*;

(f)   have his race, culture, religion and background taken into account in care proceedings, s 1 CA 1989 and para 4 *Principles and Practice*;

(g)   consult a solicitor of her own if of sufficient age and understanding;

(h)   develop a sense of identity, para 19 *Principles and Practice*;

(i)   grow to independence, para 26 *Principles and Practice*;

(j)   to live in peace and safety, free from abuse, para 3 *Principles and Practice*.

7.6.6 Rights of parents of a child in care

Parents (with parental responsibility or not) and those with parental responsibility for a child in care, have the right to:

(a)   consultation when plans are being made, para 2.53 *Residential Care*, paras 7 and para 10 *Principles and Practice*;

(b)   information on where their child is being kept, Sch 2, para 15(2) Children Act;

(c)   reasonable contact with their child s 34 Children Act, paras 14-16, *Principles and Practice*;

(d)   receive financial or practical assistance with travelling to see their child Sch 2, para 16;

(e)   be a party to written agreements about the child's placement *Residential Care*, para 2.63;

(f)   participate actively in planning for the child's future, *Residential Care*, para 2.49, which states: 'The child's family, parents, grandparents, and other relatives involved with the child should be invited to participate actively in planning and to make their views known.

If the local authority departs from the care plan in breach of the child's ECHR rights, under HRA 1998 ss 7 & 8 the court may grant relief or remedy.

7.7 The PLO: Principles, 'Split Hearings', Issues Resolution, Interim and Final Hearings

7.7.1 Main principles of the PLO

In para 3.1 of the PLO, the main principles underlying court case management in Public Law Proceedings are –

(1) judicial continuity: each case will be allocated to one or two case management judges or case managers, who will be responsible for every case management stage through to the Final Hearing and, in relation to the High Court or county court, one of whom may be – and where possible should be - the judge who will conduct the Final Hearing;

(2) main case management tools: each case will be managed by the court by using the appropriate main case management tools;

(3) active case management: each case will be actively case managed by the court with a view at all times to furthering the overriding objective;

(4) consistency: each case will, so far as compatible with the overriding objective, be managed in a consistent way and using the standardised steps.

The case management depends on the use of:

- A timetable for the child who is the subject of the proceedings. Setting out all significant steps in the child's life that are likely to take place during the proceedings. This will include legal, health care, social care, review and other steps.

- Case Management Documentation which, under para 3.5. of the PLO will include:

    (i)   Application form;

    (ii) Supplementary Form PLO1;

    (iii) Schedule of Proposed Findings;

    (iv) Allocation Record and the Timetable for the Child;

    (v)   Case Analysis and Recommendations provided by Cafcass or Cafcass Cymru;

    (vi) Local Authority Case Summary;

    (vii) Other Parties' Case Summaries;

    (viii) Draft Case Management Orders.

- Case Management Record under para 3.7. this will include:

    (i)   the Supplementary Form PLO1 which will be the index of documents on the Record;

    (ii)   in care and supervision proceedings, any Letter Before Proceedings and any related subsequent correspondence confirming the Local Authority's position to parents and others with parental responsibility for the child;

    (iii)   the Case Management Documentation;

    (iv)   Standard Directions on Issue and on First Appointment;

    (v)   the Draft Case Management Orders approved by the court.

7.7.2 The 4 stages of the Public Law Outline are:

- Stage 1 – Issue of application, allocation record, and pre-proceedings checklist and *First Appointment.*
- Stage 2 – Advocates Meeting, Draft Case Management Order, and *Case Management Conference.*
- Stage 3 – Advocates Meeting, Draft Case Management Order, Issues *Resolution Hearing.*
- Stage 4 – *Final Hearing* and directions.

Often, cases present issues of fact which require identification, clarification, or determination.

7.7.3 Split hearings

Before the PLO came into force, the term 'split hearings' (meaning the separate hearings in which the process of fact finding, threshold criteria and subsequent disposal were decided in stages) was commonly used. 'Fact finding' hearings are used to clarify and adjudicate on factual matters in dispute, for example in cases of sexual or physical abuse, identification of the perpetrator, and are split off from the final hearing of the case. Guidance was provided in a plethora of case law on the use of split hearings, e.g. in *Re S (Care Proceedings: Split hearing)* [1996] 2FLR 773; *Re Y and K (Split Hearing: Evidence)* [2003] EWCA Civ 669; [2003] 2FLR 273 and *Re P (Care Proceedings: Split Hearing)* [2007] EWCA Civ 1265; [2008] Fam Law 202.

Now that the PLO is in force, we may hear more of the stages of the PLO and the 'issues resolution hearing' instead. Whatever the terminology, their purpose will be to clarify or resolve salient issues before the final hearing, consider the care plan and review the timetable for the child.

7.7.4   PLO Checklists

Pre-proceedings checklist

For a detailed and authoritative explanation of the PLO see (Pressdee et al 2008) *The Public Law Outline: The Court Companion.*

Documents to be disclosed from the Local Authority's files:

* Previous court orders & judgments/reasons
* Any relevant Assessment Materials
    - Initial and core assessments
    - Section 7 & 37 reports
    - Relatives & friends materials (e.g. a genogram)
* Other relevant Reports & Records
    - Single, joint or inter-agency materials (e.g. health & education/ Home Office & Immigration documents)
    - Records of discussions with the family
    - Key LA minutes & records for the child (including Strategy Discussion Record)
* Pre-existing care plans (e.g. child in need plan, looked after child plan & child protection plan)
* Social Work Chronology
* Letters Before Proceedings

Documents to be prepared for the proceedings:

* Schedule of Proposed Findings
* Initial Social Work Statement
* Care Plan
* Allocation Record & Timetable for the Child

Stage 1 Issue and the first appointment

Objectives: To ensure compliance with pre-proceedings checklist; to allocate proceedings; to obtain the information necessary for initial case management at the FA

On Day 1:

* The LA files:
    - Application Form

- Supplementary Form PLO1

- Checklist documents

- Court officer issues application
- Court nominates case manager(s)
- Court gives standard directions on issue including:

   - Pre-proceedings checklist compliance

   - Allocate and/or transfer

   - Appoint children's guardian

   - Appoint solicitor for the child

   - Case Analysis for FA

   - Invite OS to act for protected persons (non subject children & incapacitated adults)

   - List FA by Day 6

   - Make arrangements for contested hearing (if necessary)

By Day 3

- Allocation of a children's guardian expected
- LA serves the Application Form, Supplementary Form PLO1 and the Checklist Documents on parties
- Parties notify LA & court of need for a contested hearing
- Court makes arrangements for a contested hearing
- Initial case management by Court including:

   - Confirm Timetable for the Child

   - Confirm allocation or transfer

   - Identify additional parties & representation (including allocation of children's guardian)

   - Identify "Early Final Hearing" cases

   - Scrutinise Care Plan

- Court gives standard directions on FA including:

   - Case Analysis and Recommendations for Stages 2 & 3

   - LA Case Summary

   - Other Parties' Case Summaries

   - Parties' initial witness statements

   - For the Advocates' Meeting

- List CMC or (if appropriate) an Early Final Hearing

- Upon transfer

Stage 2 Case Management Conference

ADVOCATES' MEETING

No later than 2 days before CMC

Objectives: To prepare the Draft Case Management Order; to identify experts and draft questions for them

Tasks:

- Consider all other parties' Case Summaries and Case Analysis and Recommendations
- Identify proposed experts and draft questions in accordance with Experts Practice Direction
- Draft Case Management Order
- Notify court of need for a contested hearing
- File Draft Case Management Order with the case manager/case management judge by 11am one working day before the CMC

CMC

No later than day 45

Objectives: To identify issue(s); to give full case management directions

Tasks:

- Detailed case management by the court
  - Scrutinise compliance with directions
  - Confirm Timetable for the Child
  - Identify key issue(s)
  - Confirm allocation or transfer
  - Consider case management directions in the Draft Case Management Order
  - Scrutinise Care Plan
  - Check compliance with Experts Practice Direction
- Court issues Case Management Order
- Court lists IRH and, where necessary, a warned period for Final Hearing

Stage 3 Issues Resolution Hearing

ADVOCATES' MEETING

Between 2 and 7 days before the IRH

Objective: To prepare or update the Draft Case Management Order

- Consider all other parties' Case Summaries and Case Analysis and Recommendations
- Draft Case Management Order
- Notify court of need for a contested hearing/time for oral evidence to be given
- File Draft Case Management Order with the case manager/case management judge by 11am one working day before the IRH

IRH

Between 16 & 25 weeks

Objectives: To resolve and narrow issue(s); to identify any remaining key issues

- Identification by the court of the key issue(s) (if any) to be determined
- Final case management by the court:
    - Scrutinise compliance with directions
    - Consider case management directions in the Draft Case Management Order
    - Scrutinise Care Plan
    - Give directions for Hearing documents:
    - Threshold agreement or facts/issues remaining to be determined
    - Final Evidence & Care Plan
    - Case Analysis and Recommendations
    - Witness templates
    - Skeleton arguments
    - Judicial reading list/reading time/judgment writing time
    - Time estimate
    - Bundles Practice Direction compliance
    - List or confirm Hearing
- Court issues Case Management Order

Stage 4   The Final hearing

In accordance with the Timetable for the Child

Objective: To determine remaining issues

*   All file & serve updated case management documents & bundle
*   Draft final order(s) in approved form
*   Judgment/reasons
*   Disclose documents as required after hearing

For a detailed discussion of the PLO, case management tools, and documentation, with useful flowcharts, see Hershman and McFarlane, pages C 117-123 paras 1031-1040.

7.8 Assessments and care planning

Only when the threshold grounds (s 31 criteria) are established, will the court go on to consider what, if any, order to make.

No care order may be made unless the court has first considered a care plan submitted by the local authority s 31(3A) and see LAC 99(29).

The next task for the court, therefore, once the s 31 criteria are satisfied, is to consider the circumstances of the child in the context of the underlying principles of the CA 1989, consider the welfare checklist, and to decide whether the making of an order is necessary in the best interests of the child and, if so, which order would be the most appropriate in all the circumstances of the case.

In the past, some local authorities were lax about their care plans and the courts were asked to make care orders 'on trust' that the authority would do the right thing for the child. Now the courts subject care plans to very careful scrutiny. Home Office Circular LAC (99)29 and NAFWC 1/222 in Wales provides a structure for care plans. Evidence should be called in support of care plans, and known placement details made available to the court. Note that, once the care order is made the court can no longer control events. In *Re S(Minors) (Care Order: Implementation of Care Plan)*, and *Re W (Care Order: Adequacy of Care Plan)* [2002] UKHL 10; [2002] 1FLR 815, the House of Lords affirmed the right of local authorities to discharge their responsibility under care orders without interference from the courts. However, the role of the Independent Reporting Office and Local Authority Care Reviews should protect the interests of the child.

In order to assist the court, under the PLO, the applicant is expected to have provided at least a chronology, appropriate evidence including social work statement(s), detailed care plan(s), assessment materials, other relevant reports and documents, and an allocation record and timetable in which the proposed arrangements for the child are set out for the consideration of the court.

See Chapter 16 below for discussion of assessments within the new Assessment Framework and Guidance, and further information on care planning.

If the grounds are satisfied, much of the court's time will then be spent on considering proportionality, and assessment and discussion of the timetable and care plan, in order to make the best decision for the child's short and long term future.

7.9 Effects of supervision order

A supervision order places the child under the supervision of a local authority or a probation officer. The duties and powers of the supervising officer are set out in s 35 and Sch 3, including a duty 'to advise, assist and befriend' the child. The supervising officer does not acquire parental responsibility for the child. The sanction for failure to co-operate with supervision is an application to discharge the order and to substitute something else, possibly a care order, see 8.9.3 below.

Directions may be made within supervision orders binding those responsible for the child and also the child to attend activities or live at specified places (see below, 7.9.3). They subsist for the duration of the supervision order or such lesser period as the court may specify

A supervision order is possible within criminal proceedings on a finding of guilt against a juvenile offender, under s 7(7) of the Children and Young Persons Act 1969. Those orders may contain a direction that a child lives in local authority accommodation for a period of up to six months, but note that the criteria in s 31 do not have to be met before a 'criminal supervision order' is made, and also that a criminal court cannot make a care order. Criminal supervision orders are not discussed in this book, because they are different from orders made under s 31. However, a child in local authority accommodation under a criminal supervision order must have the same rights under Vol 4 of the *Guidance, Residential Care*, as a child living away from home under a Children Act care or supervision order.

7.9.1 Interim orders

If a care or supervision application is adjourned, the court can make an interim order, s 38(1). In the context of interim care or supervision orders, the court can make directions for medical or psychiatric assessment which a child of sufficient age and understanding may refuse, s 38(6) and (7); and the court may also make an exclusion requirement under s 38(A), ordering a named person to leave and/or excluding them from entering a dwelling house or defined geographical area in which the child lives. A power of arrest may be attached to the exclusion order, enforceable by the police, s 38(A)(5)–(9).

Where the court has power to impose an exclusion requirement in an interim care order, undertakings may be accepted from the relevant person, s 38(B). However, undertakings, although they are enforceable as an order of the court, cannot be coupled with a power of arrest.

Section 38(3) provides that if there is an application for care, but the court decides to make a residence order (for limited duration) instead of a care order, then the court must also make an interim supervision order unless it is satisfied that the child's welfare will be adequately safeguarded without one.

7.9.2 Duration of care and supervision

A supervision order may last for up to one year, s 91(3) and Sch 3, para 6. It may be for shorter duration if so ordered by the court. A supervision order may also be extended by the court on a subsequent hearing for a further period or periods of up to a year, to a maximum of three years from the date it was first made, Sch 3, para 6(3) and (4). Section 1 principles apply (see Chapter 2 above and see *Wakefield MDC UT* [2008] EWCA Civ 199; [2008] Fam Law 485).

7.9.3 Directions in supervision orders

Directions to the child

The court may embody in the order specific requirements with which the child is to comply; and/or a general term along the lines that 'the child must comply with the directions given from time to time by the supervisor'. The supervisor then has a certain amount of leeway about the directions given, provided they fall within the parameters set in Sch 3, para 2.

These are:

(a)   to live at a place or places specified;

(b)   to present himself to a person or persons specified for a period or periods specified;

(c)   to participate in specified activities on dates and at times specified.

Directions to a 'responsible person'

A responsible person is defined in Sch 3, para 1 as 'a person who has parental responsibility for the child, and any other person with whom the child is living'.

Under Sch 3, with the consent of the responsible person, the court can include in the order a number of requirements:

(a) to take reasonable steps to ensure the child complies with the directions of the supervisor under Sch 3, para 2 (that is, to live at a specified place, present himself to a person specified on a specific day and to participate in activities);

(b) to take all reasonable steps to ensure the supervised child complies with directions regarding medical and psychiatric examinations (Sch 3, paras 3-5);

(c) that he or she comply with direction of supervisor 'to attend at a place specified in the directions for the purpose of taking part in activities so specified'.

A supervision order may also direct the responsible person to keep the supervisor informed of change of address, and to allow the supervisor to visit the child where they are living.

The responsible person may be directed to ensure the child complies with the supervisor's programme, giving the order a better chance of success. The adult may be asked to attend a treatment centre, to benefit the family and enable the child to remain at home.

The county court has no jurisdiction to accept undertakings in care or supervision cases, *Re B (A Minor) (Supervision Order: Parental Undertaking)* [1996] 1 FLR 676.

The court has no jurisdiction to specify the activities in which the responsible person (with their consent) is to participate. This is for the supervisor to arrange. The supervisor can therefore direct a sex offender to have treatment *Re H (Minors) (Terms of Supervision Orders)* [1994] Fam Law 486.

The court may authorise medical or psychiatric examination, and also direct attendance by the child and/or carers for medical or psychiatric examination of the child, or, if necessary, in-patient or outpatient treatment, which a child of sufficient understanding has a right to refuse (see Chapter 12 below, and Sch 3, paras 4 and 5). Although the supervisor has the power to direct attendance by the child for medical or psychiatric examination or assessment, only the court can authorise medical or psychological examination. Before making these directions, the court must know that satisfactory arrangements have been, or can be, made for the treatment proposed. This implies that the practitioners concerned have indicated that they agree to carry it out. If the child has sufficient understanding, their consent is also required.

If a health practitioner is unwilling to continue treatment of the child, or the directions need altering because of any of the following circumstances:

(a) the treatment should be extended beyond the period specified in the order;

(b) different treatment is required;

(c) the child is not susceptible to treatment; or

(d) no further treatment is required;

he must submit a written report to the supervisor, who will then have to put that report back to the court for revision of the directions, Sch 3, para 5 (6)–(7).

7.9.4 Enforcement

If there is a direction that the supervisor visits the child, and this is prevented, then the supervisor may bring the matter back to court for a warrant for a police officer to 'assist the supervisor to exercise these powers, using reasonable force if necessary', s 102(1). Other conditions cannot specifically be enforced, but their breach can be justification for bringing the matter back before the court for an application to discharge the supervision order, to seek a care order, or for a different order to be made.

The Court of Appeal has held that if a local authority wants to substitute care for supervision, it needs a specific application for a care order and the s 31 threshold criteria must be proved in support of the care application, *Re A (Minor) (Supervision Extension)* [1995] 2 FCR 114, CA.

7.10 Removal of child from care

Local authorities have a duty to look after and maintain children subject to care orders while they are in force, s 33(1). A parent, or anyone else, may not remove a child from the care of the local authority without leave of the court. Removal of a child without permission of the local authority or leave of the court, keeping a child away from local authority care, or inciting a child to run away or stay away, is a criminal offence of child abduction under s 49.

Note that if children are accommodated on a voluntary basis by a local authority (under ss 20-24), the situation is different in that they may be removed at any time by a person with parental responsibility for them. A local authority has no power to keep a child in voluntary accommodation where there is a person with parental responsibility ready and willing to look after the child.

7.11 Variation, discharge and appeals

Care orders cease when the child reaches the age of 18, or earlier by order of the court (s 91(2)).

Supervision orders cease when directed by the court or on effluxion of time.

7.11.1 Variation and discharge

Applicant

A care or supervision order may be varied or discharged on the application of:

(a) any person with parental responsibility for the child;

(b) the child (who does not need leave of the court);

(c) in the case of supervision, the supervisor;

(d) in the case of a care order, the local authority with the responsibility for the child.

The application needs to be on form C1. Leave, if required, is on form C2, with a draft application in form C1 attached. The court should be that which made the original order. Other courts may accept the application if made with good reason.

Once made, the application may only be withdrawn with leave of the court, see r 5(1) FPC(CA)R 1991 and r 4.5(1)FPR 1991.

If the court discharges a care order it can order supervision, without having to re-prove the s 31(2) criteria, ss 39(4) and (5).

Following an unsuccessful application to discharge a care order, there is no further application without leave within six months, s 91(5) CA 1989. Under s 91(14) the court can order no further applications without leave, but should use this power sparingly, see *Re G* [1996] 2 FCR 1.

Notice

Applications for discharge should be made on notice. The applicant should serve each person entitled to notice with form C6A, with the date and time of the hearing endorsed on it, at least seven days before first directions or hearing. See r 4(3) FPC(CA)R 1991 and FPR 1991 r 4.4(3). Those entitled to notice are the same as for the original application.

Respondents

Those who are entitled to be respondents should be served with a notice of the proceedings in form C6, together with a draft of the application on form C1, at least seven days before the first directions or hearing. See r 4(1)(b) FPC(CA)R 1991 and r 4.4(1)(b) FPR 1991.

Those entitled to be respondents are those who were entitled to be, or were, respondents in the original application.

7.11.2 Appeals

Appeals against decisions concerning care orders lie from the family proceedings court to the High Court, and from the county court and the High Court to the Court of Appeal, see Chapter 17 below.

On refusal to make a care order, or on discharge, the court has power to make a care order pending appeal, s 40(1) and (2); or to declare that the order appealed shall not take effect pending appeal, s 40(3). If the court of first instance refuses to make a care order pending appeal, the appeal court may make an interim care under s 38 Children Act 1989.

7.12 Effects of the Human Rights Act 1998 on care and supervision proceedings

Public authorities must comply with the Human Rights Act 1998 and the European Convention for the Protection of Human Rights and Fundamental Freedoms (ECHR). Any acts by public authorities incompatible with these may be challenged by complaint, appeal or judicial review.

Failure to act is a ground for complaint or challenge, see ss 6 and 7 of the Human Rights Act 1998. Section 22(4) allows retrospective challenge of acts which occurred before the Human Rights Act came into force.

Article 6 (right to a fair trial) may provide an opportunity to encourage the involvement of children and families in decision making within care planning.

Article 8 of the ECHR gives the right to respect for family life, home and correspondence. It may affect the interpretation of current law on contact, family involvement in care plans and care of children, post-adoption contact and the rights of children and their parents in the context of residential care. Watch the case law as it unfolds in these areas of child protection, since Article 8 provides an additional potential ground for appeal against local authority and court decisions and to challenge failures to act by public authorities.

Since April 2009 the family courts are now open to the media (with judicial control), and this may have an influence on future child and family litigation in ways that have not yet been anticipated.

8 Secure Accommodation

Local authorities have a duty to provide accommodation for children in need in circumstances specified in s 20 CA 1989 and may otherwise provide accommodation to safeguard or promote the welfare of a child. Secure accommodation is defined in s 25(1) CA 1989 as 'accommodation provided for the purpose of restricting liberty'.

Currently, the law relating to secure accommodation is complex, and in need of clarification. Children aged between 13 and 18 can be placed in secure accommodation for a variety of reasons. They may have committed a criminal offence and need to have their liberty restricted for their own safety or that of others. Orders made in these circumstances are called 'secure orders', to distinguish them from the orders made in civil cases. Children being detained for certain grave crimes are not eligible for secure orders, see 8.1.1. below.

A child who is looked after by a local authority, or subject to a care order, may be kept in secure accommodation by the power given by a court order under s 25 CA 1989. In certain circumstances, a child may be kept in secure accommodation by the consent of parents or those with parental responsibility.

Secure accommodation is currently governed by s 25 CA 1989, by the Children (Secure Accommodation) Regulations 1991 SI 1991/1505 (the 'Secure Accommodation Regulations'); the Children (Secure Accommodation) (No 2) Regulations 1991 SI 1991/2034 and by the *Children Act 1989 Regulations and Guidance* Vol 4 *Residential Care ('Residential Care')*, Chapter 8, pp 118-29, and *Children Act 1989 Regulations and Guidance* Vol 1. *Court Orders (2008)*.

Secure accommodation should be based on the needs of the child, never because of inadequacies of staffing or resources in residential accommodation, nor because a child is being a nuisance. It may never be used as a punishment, see *Children Act 1989 Regulations and Guidance* Vol 1 *Court Orders (2008)* at paras 5.1 – 5.3, and *Children Act 1989 Regulations and Guidance* Vol 4 *Residential Care ('Residential Care')* para 8.5.

A child below the age of 13 years may not be kept in secure accommodation without authority of the Secretary of State, reg 13(4), Secure Accommodation Regulations. Children over 16 years of age, may not be kept in secure accommodation and wards of court may only be placed in secure accommodation with a direction from the wardship judge.

Secure accommodation is not incompatible with the ECHR 1950. The Convention allows minors to be detained by lawful order for the purpose of educational provision. The courts must ensure that any secure accommodation order makes educational provision. Failure to do so would be in breach of the ECHR, see *Re K (Secure Accommodation Order: Right to Liberty)* [2001] 1 FLR 526.

8.1 Restricting liberty with a secure accommodation order

The effect of a secure accommodation order is restrict a child's liberty. Local authorities should pay careful regard to the guidance in their use of restriction of liberty. There is a distinction between placing a child in an environment (secure unit), from which he cannot run away and in which he is safeguarded; and the temporary restriction of a child's liberty, for example, locking him in a room. There is a type of restraint, colloquially called 'pindown', formerly used in residential care, in which children who are disruptive or disobedient are punished by isolation in locked rooms, possibly with the additional deprivation of stimuli (for example, removal of their radios, TVs, writing and reading materials, sometimes even clothes), for periods varying from hours to days. Some residential children's homes even had specially adapted rooms set aside for this purpose. This type of punishment probably developed from a more moderate form of behavioural training called 'time out' to quieten overactive or disruptive children. 'Pindown' is a very severe form of `time out', and has been much criticised in recent years because of the potentially emotionally abusive effect it can have on the child concerned. *Residential Care* at para 8.10 emphasises that 'any practice or measure which prevents a child from leaving a room or building of his own free will may be deemed by the court to be a restriction of liberty'. In the community homes system, the liberty of children may only be restricted in secure accommodation approved by the Secretary of State. There are other secure units outside the community homes system, for example, Youth Treatment Centres, which are covered by s 25.

In *Residential Care* at para 8.14 is clearly stated that:

> ... subject to the exclusions mentioned in para 8.13 [Children detained under the Mental Health Act 1983] ... no child, other than one looked after by a local authority who is accommodated in the circumstances defined, may have his liberty restricted unless the statutory criteria for

the use of secure accommodation in s 25(1) CA 1989 applies. This applies equally to any proposed short term placement of the child in a locked room for 'time out' or seclusion purposes. The maximum period such a child may be kept in secure accommodation without the authority of the court is 72 hours, whether consecutively or in aggregate in any period of 28 days.

So, we have to conclude that 'time out' as a behavioural approach to child care is still contemplated, but is now subject to stricter regulation.

Safeguards

(a) Restriction of liberty should constitute a last resort, para 5(1) of *Court Orders*.

(b) Secure placements should be only for so long as necessary.

(c) Regular inspection and review by:

(i) Secretary of State (to approve secure unit);

(ii) Social Services Inspectorate (general running and facilities);

(iii) Department of Education (educational facilities);

(iv) Regional Placements Committee (placements);

(v) Secure Accommodation Review Committee (resources).

(f) Time limits on the duration of secure accommodation orders.

(d) Care plans required by court on review of the orders.

(d) Each child has the right to an independent visitor.

(d) The 'three wise men (or women)'.

The local authority keeping a child in a secure unit must appoint at least three people, one of whom must not be a local authority employee, to review the placement within one month, and thereafter at three-monthly intervals. The task of these three is to ensure that the criteria justifying secure accommodation still applies, and that the placement is necessary, and no other description of accommodation is appropriate. See reg 15, Secure Accommodation Regulations. The local authority must keep good case records, with details listed in reg 17. The safeguards in s 25 also cover children accommodated by the National Health Service Trusts and local education authorities.

8.1.1 Criminal cases (Secure orders)

In criminal proceedings, a child may be remanded or bailed to local authority accommodation under s 23 of the Children and Young Persons Act 1969. Once there, the child may behave in such a way that there is concern that the child may abscond, or injure himself or others. If this concern is justified, then the local authority or other named persons (see 8.4 below) may seek a secure order. The complication in the law at the moment is that the routes to the order and the rules applicable vary according to the court to which the child has been remanded. The grounds for the application in each of these circumstances are set out in 8.3 below, and procedures at 8.4. There is an excellent explanatory chart in *Children Law and Practice* (Hershman and McFarlane) Vol 1, section G at para [396].

Children detained pursuant to s 53 of the Children and Young Persons Act 1933, (punishment for certain grave crimes) may not be subject to a secure order.

Juveniles may be detained by the police under circumstances specified in s 38 of the Police and Criminal Evidence Act 1984 ('PACE') and under s 38(6), the juvenile shall be moved to local authority accommodation unless the custody officer certifies that either it is impracticable to do so, or in the case of a juvenile over 12 years old, no secure accommodation is available and other local authority accommodation would not be adequate to protect the public from serious harm from him. Remands of juveniles to local authority accommodation by the police in this way are covered by the provisions of s 25 CA 1989. There are also safeguards for young people arrested, protecting their interests in detention and during questioning.

Under s 130 of the Criminal Justice Act 1988, if juvenile offenders are remanded to local authority accommodation, and placed in secure units, their time so spent will be deducted from their eventual custodial sentence. See also Local Authority Circular LAC (88) 23, which reminds local authorities to keep accurate records of the duration of detention of children in secure units for the sentencing court.

8.1.2 Use of secure accommodation in civil cases

Paragraph 8.6 of *Residential Care* emphasises the local authority duty to 'take reasonable steps to avoid the need for children within their area to be placed in secure accommodation'. This duty is set out in Sch 2, para 7(c) CA 1989, but also to 'encourage children within their area not to commit criminal offences', para 7(b). Placement decisions should be taken at a senior level, not lower than Assistant Director, accountable to the Director of Social Services. The placement should be part of the authority's overall plan for the child, and to safeguard and promote the child's welfare, s 22 CA 1989.

8.2 How long can a child be kept in secure accommodation?

8.2.1   Where no court order made

Without the authority of the court, a child may only have his liberty restricted for up to 72 hours, either consecutively or in aggregate within any period of 28 consecutive days, reg 10(1) Secure Accommodation Regulations.   Where a child has been placed in local authority accommodation on a voluntary basis under s 20(1) CA 1989, a person with parental responsibility can remove the child at any time, s 20(8), unless the exceptions in s 20(9) apply. This includes removal from secure accommodation.

8.2.2   Secure order (child on remand in a criminal case)

Where the child has been remanded by a criminal court, the duration is for the period of the remand, with a maximum order of 28 days, reg 13 Secure Accommodation Regulations.

Regulation 10(2) gives an exception where, if the court authorises secure accommodation for less than 28 days, on the day when the court order expires, the 28 day period mentioned in reg 10(1) starts running afresh from that day, ignoring any time spent in secure accommodation before the court order. Reg 10(3) gives special provisions for days either side of public holidays by granting a limited extension of the 72 hour time limit.

8.2.3   Civil cases and children not on criminal remand - secure accommodation orders

If the child is not on remand, or committed to the Crown Court, then the maximum period is:

*   up to three months on the first application, reg 11, and
*   up to six months on subsequent applications, reg 12.

The period of detention runs from the date the order was made, not the date the child was actually placed in the unit, see *Re B (Minor) (Secure Accommodation)* [1994] 2 FLR 707.

Any period in the secure unit before a secure accommodation order is made should be deducted from this. *C (Minor) v Humberside CC and Another* [1995] 1 FCR 110. The justices making a care order had no power to order that a child kept in secure accommodation for a month should then be kept in the secure unit for a further three months.

In the case of *In Re W (Minor) (Secure Accommodation Order)* [1993] 1 FLR 692 it was held that the court should consider the shortest appropriate period, rather than order the maximum period available as a matter of course.

If the criteria for detention in secure accommodation cease to apply, the child must be released, *LM v Essex CC* [1999] 1 FLR 988.

8.2.4 Adjournments

If there is an adjournment of an application for secure accommodation, then, under s 25(5) CA 1989, the court may permit the child to be kept secure during the adjournment. There is here an obvious risk of getting the order sought by the back door, perhaps without adequate proof of its necessity, particularly if the adjournment is for further evidence to become available.

In the case of *Birmingham City Council v M* [2008] EWHC 1085 Fam, the court held that the court could not adjourn a secure accommodation application solely in order to keep the children's guardian and solicitor engaged in the case and supporting the child, and that if the adjournment was not justified (e.g. to obtain further information or for reasons of procedural fairness), then the court should hold the substantive hearing.

8.3 Grounds for application

8.3.1 Children remanded in criminal cases

Where a child has been remanded by a criminal court to local authority accommodation, under s 23 of the Children and Young Persons Act 1969, or bailed to reside in local authority accommodation, he may be the subject of an application for secure accommodation under s 25 CA 1989.

If the young person was remanded by a youth court, then the application under s 25 CA 1989 should be made to the youth court, and if remanded by magistrates, application should be made to the magistrates.

If he was remanded by the Crown Court then application should be made to the family proceedings court.

Section 23 of the Children and Young Persons Act 1969 applies to children who are:

(a) charged with or convicted of an offence which would carry a sentence of 14 years or more for a person over 21 years old;

(b) charged with or convicted of an offence of violence, or who have a previous conviction for violence;

(c) detained under s 38(6) of PACE 1984.

These children, if remanded to local authority accommodation, are subject to reg 6(2) of the Secure Accommodation Regulations, which provides that a child may not be kept in secure accommodation unless it appears that any accommodation other than that provided for the purpose of restricting his liberty is inappropriate because:

(a) the child is likely to abscond from such accommodation;

(b) the child is likely to injure himself or other people if he is kept in any such accommodation.

Note that the likelihood of significant harm is omitted in this regulation.

If the criteria are satisfied, then the order must be made. The welfare of the child is not the paramount consideration in this situation .

The criteria for children in civil cases is slightly different, see 8.3.2. below.

8.3.2 Children in civil cases

Children accommodated in residential care homes, nursing homes, mental nursing homes, or accommodated by health authorities or National Health Service Trusts, are subject to the provisions of s 25 CA 1989.

Section 25 CA 1989 provides that if:

(a) (i) the child has a history of absconding and is likely to abscond from any other description of accommodation; and

(ii) if he absconds he is likely to suffer significant harm; or

(b) that if he is kept in any other description of accommodation, he is likely to injure himself or others,

the child can be placed in local authority accommodation by the court.

In the case of *Re M (A Minor) (Secure Accommodation Order)* [1995] 2 FCR 373, the welfare of the child was held by the court to be relevant, but not paramount in s 25 proceedings, and therefore application of the welfare checklist, although useful, was not obligatory.

A child may be placed in a secure unit under s 25(1) to prevent her injuring another child, which may be inconsistent with putting the welfare of the secured child first. The court's duty mirrors that of the local authority under s 20(1)(b) CA 1989. The court must ascertain whether the s 25 conditions are satisfied, and if so, to make the order if this accords with the duty of the local authority to safeguard and promote the welfare of the child. The children's guardian will assist the court in deciding these questions: *Re M (Secure Accommodation Order)* [1995] Fam 108; [1995] 3 All ER 407; [1995] 1 FLR 418.

If the child is voluntarily accommodated by the local authority, i.e. not subject to a care order) a person with parental responsibility may remove them from the secure accommodation at any time, see ss 20(8), 20(9) and 25(9) CA 1989.

8.4 Practice and procedure

Secure accommodation orders are not included in the definition of 'family proceedings' in s 8 CA 1989, but because s 92(2) says that 'all proceedings under the Act shall be treated as family proceedings in relation to magistrates' courts', this means that in the Family Proceedings Court, s 25 applications are included. The 'menu' of orders available in family proceedings is therefore open to the court, including s 8 orders and others which the court can make of its own volition (see Figure 8, below, pp 124-25).

8.4.1 Application

Where a child is being looked after by a local authority (even if the child is accommodated by another body) that local authority should be the applicant for the order. In other circumstances, other potential applicants include those who are providing accommodation for the child, that is:

* local authority;
* health authority or NHS Trust;
* local education authority;
* person carrying on residential home, nursing home, or mental nursing home.

Once made, an application may only be withdrawn with leave of the court.

8.4.2 Forms

The application should be made on form C1 together with form C20 in accordance with Sch 1 to the Family Proceedings Courts (Children

Act) Rules 1991 (FPC(CA)R), and App 1 Family Proceedings Rules 1991 (FPR).

If the application is made to the High Court in wardship, it should be by summons and the ward should be named as a party, r 5(5) FPR 1991 as amended by the Family Proceedings (Amendment) Rules 1992 SI 1992/456.

8.4.3 Venue

Secure accommodation orders can be made at any level of the court. They can be made in criminal proceedings at the youth court or at a higher level of criminal court; and in the Family Proceedings Court or the county court or High Court in the course of other proceedings.

8.4.4 Respondents

Respondents should be served with a copy of the application in form C1 with C20, with the date of hearing or directions, and notice of the proceedings with the date and place of hearing, FPC(CA)R, r 4(1)(b), and r 4.4(1)(b) FPR 1991.

Service should be one day before the hearing; r 4(4) FPC(CA)R and r 4.4(4) FPR 1991.

Certain people are automatically respondents to the application:

(a) those believed to have parental responsibility for the child;

(b) those who had parental responsibility prior to the care order, if one is in force;

(c) the child.

Others may be joined as respondents, and automatic respondents may be removed by direction of the court. See r 7(1) FPC(CA)R and r 4.7(1) FPR 1991.

If the application is made to the High Court in wardship, the ward should be named as a party, r 5(5) FPR as amended by the Family Proceedings (Amendment) Rules 1992 SI 1992/456.

8.4.5 Notice

Applications for secure accommodation must be made on one day's notice, r 4(4) FPC(CA)R, and r 4.4(4) FPR 1991.

The following people are entitled to notice of the proceedings, with the date, time and place of the hearing:

(a)   a local authority providing accommodation for the child;

(b)   any person with whom the child was living at the time proceedings were commenced;

(c)   person providing a refuge for the child under s 51 CA 1989.

Schedule 2 col (iv) FPC(CA)R and App 3 col (iii) FPR 1991.

Rule 4(3) FPC(CA)R, and r 4.4(3) FPR 1991 provide that if a child is placed in a secure unit in a community home, and there is an application to keep the child there, certain people need to be informed as soon as practicable:

(a)   the child's parents;

(b)   any person with parental responsibility for the child;

(c)   the child's independent visitor;

(d)   any other person the local authority considers should be told.

8.4.6 Service

Service is effected on a solicitor for a party by delivery at his office, by first class post at the office or through the DX, or by fax to the office.

Service on a party who has no solicitor is by delivery to that party personally, or by delivery of first class post to his address, r 8 FPC(CA) R, and r 4.8 FPR 1991.

Service on a child may be through her solicitor, or the children's guardian, or, with leave of the court, service on the child herself, r 8 (4) FPC(CA)R, and r 4.8(4) FPR 1991.

The time for service may be abridged by the court, or waived altogether, see r 8(8) FPC(CA)R and r 4.8(8) FPR 1991.

8.5 Role of the Children's Guardian

These proceedings are 'specified proceedings' within the meaning of s 41 CA 1989 and therefore a children's guardian must be appointed by the court unless it is of the opinion that it is unnecessary to do so in order to safeguard the child's interests. This is a protective measure intended to ensure that children in secure units have had their wishes and feelings made known to the court, and that the court has been advised of the most appropriate way forward in the best interests of the child. Children who are accommodated on a voluntary basis under s 20(1) CA 1989 are also safeguarded by this provision.

8.6 Contact

Children in secure units have the right to reasonable contact with members of their family, as children in care (see above, 7.6.4. and below, 12.5. Since a s 25 application in a magistrates' court amounts to 'family proceedings' under s 8 CA 1989, provided there is no care order in force, it is possible for the court to make a s 8 contact order to run alongside the secure accommodation order. A s 8 contact order can also co-exist with a supervision order. If the child is in care, then a s 34 care contact order may be made if necessary.

8.7 Rights of the child

These are:

*   three persons to review placement, reg 15, Children (Secure Accommodation) Regulations 1991 SI 1991/1505, reg 15;
*   duty on local authority to keep detailed case records, reg 17;
*   education whilst accommodated;
*   entitlement to appropriate therapy where necessary;
*   regular inspection of the secure unit by the Social Services Inspectorate from the Department of Health, who must approve the unit;
*   inspection by the Department of Education, because children there are receiving education whilst accommodated;
*   regional placement committees, who check the resources and conditions of the unit;
*   time limits on the duration of secure accommodation orders;
*   care plans on review of the orders;
*   independent visitor;
*   consultation, and to have wishes and feelings ascertained, s 22(4) CA 1989;
*   consultation with parents and those with parental responsibility, s 22(4) CA 1989; and
*   'free' legal aid to be represented on s 25 application.

8.7.1 Legal aid

Section 99 CA 1989 amends the Legal Aid Act 1988 ensuring legal aid is granted to a child subject to a s 25 Children Act application, who wishes to be legally represented. Legal aid is 'free', that is, non-means and non-merits tested, available on completion of form CLA5A by the solicitor. The court may not make a secure accommodation order on an unrepresented child. The only exception is where the child has been informed of her right to apply for legal aid, and having been given the opportunity to do so, has failed to apply or refused to do so, s 25(6) Children Act.

8.8 Appeals and the Human Rights Act 1998

Section 94 CA 1989 makes provision for appeals to the High Court against decisions or refusals to authorise applications for the restriction of liberty. The placement in secure accommodation may continue whilst an appeal against authorisation is waiting to be determined. If the appeal is against a refusal to authorise the child may not be detained in a secure unit pending appeal. Appeals from the county court or High Court lie to the Court of Appeal.

The Human Rights Act 1998 and Art 5 of the European Convention for the Protection of Human Rights and Fundamental Freedoms (ECHR) is relevant to decisions of local authorities and the courts in secure accommodation issues. Article 5 confirms the right to liberty and security of a person and Art 8 protects the right to family life. Art 5 refers to the detention of minors for 'educational supervision' or for the purpose of 'bringing them before the competent legal authority'.

Acts of public authorities and the courts which do not comply with the Human Rights Act or the ECHR may be challenged by complaint, judicial review, or appeal. Note that past acts may also be challenged, s 22(4).

9 Education Supervision Orders

Education between 5 and 16 years is compulsory. The Education Act 1996 (the 'Education Act') combined with the provisions of s 36 and Sch 3 CA 1989, authorises prosecution of parents who fail to ensure that their child receives a proper full time education. Parents have the right to educate their children other than in school, provided that the child receives a 'proper education' as described below. The local education authority may agree, under the Education Act 1996, to help parents to arrange education otherwise than at school.

S 36(4) CA 1989 states that 'a child is being properly educated only if he is receiving efficient full time education suitable to his age, ability and aptitude, and any special educational needs he may have'. Under s 437 of the Education Act, a local education authority which is concerned about a child's education, may serve notice on parents to show that the child is being properly educated. If the parents fail to comply or to provide the required proof, then the the local education authority may serve on parents a 'school attendance order', requiring the parents to register the child at a named school. Failure to comply with this order constitutes an offence, and on prosecution, the court may direct the local education authority to apply for an education supervision order.

9.1 Effects of an education supervision order

An education supervision order, made under s 36 CA 1989 places the child under the supervision of a local education authority. These differ from supervision orders made under s 31. School refusal is no longer by itself a ground for care, but it may be evidence of neglect, lack of parental control, underlying emotional problems, or that the education system may be failing to meet the needs of the child. School refusal may, therefore, form part of the s 31 grounds, see Chapter 7 above, and *Re 0 (A Minor) (Care Order: Education Procedure)* [1992] 2 FLR 7.

CA 1989, in para 12 of Sch 3 sets out the supervisor's duty to 'advise, assist and befriend and give directions to the supervised child and to his parents', 'in such as way as will ... secure that he is properly educated'.

The supervisor should take into account the wishes and feelings of the child and parents, and directions made should be reasonable, and such that the parents and child are able to comply with them. Persistent failure to comply with directions may lead to prosecution.

Paragraph 18 of Sch 3 CA 1989 sets out the defences to a prosecution for failure to comply with a school attendance order, which includes: showing that all reasonable steps were taken to comply; or that the the directions were unreasonable; or that there was compliance with directions or requirements in a supervision order and that it was not reasonably practicable to comply with both the supervision order and the school attendance order.

Children Act 1989 Regulations and Guidance (Vol 7) discusses directions in paras 3.31-3.35. Directions might require the child to attend meetings with the supervisor or with teachers at the school to discuss progress, or cover medical assessment or examination, or assessment by a clinical psychologist. They should be confirmed in writing, and the parents informed.

Under Sch 3 para 13 CA 1989, parents lose their right to have the child educated at home, or move the child to another school, while an education supervision order is in force, and they have no right of appeal against admissions decisions.

Volume 7 is made under s 7 of the Local Authority Social Services Act 1970, and so local authorities must follow it unless there are cogent local reasons not to comply. Non-compliance is *prima facie* ground for complaint, and will have to be justified if challenged. However, note *Essex CC v B* [1993] 1 FLR 866.

9.2 Duration

The order will subsist for one year, or until the child is no longer of compulsory school age, whichever is the earlier, para 15(1) and (6), Sch 3 to CA 1989. It may be discharged earlier, on the application of the child, the parents, or the local education authority, para 17(1), Sch 3 to CA 1989.

It may be extended for up to three years if application is made within three months before the expiry date, and it can be extended more than once, para 15, Sch 3. It will cease on the making of a care order, Sch 3, para 15(6) (b).

9.3 Grounds for application

Under s 36(3) CA 1989, an order may only be made if the court is 'satisfied that the child concerned is of compulsory school age and is not being properly educated'; s 36(4) states that 'a child is being properly educated only if he is receiving efficient full time education suitable to his age, ability and aptitude, and any special educational needs he may have'.

Where a child is the subject to a school attendance order under s 437 of the Education Act which is in force but with which the child is not complying, or is a registered pupil of a school which he is not attending regularly within the meaning of s 444 of the Education Act; there is a presumption that the child is not being properly educated, see s 36(5) CA 1989.

Note that an order may not be sought in respect of a child who is already subject to a care order, s 36(6) CA 1989.

Before making an application for an education supervision order, the local education authority is required under s 36(8) CA 1989 to consult social services. Volume 7 para 3(18) requires everyone to make all reasonable efforts to resolve a problem of poor school attendance without the use of legal sanctions: 'Many attendance difficulties can be overcome by sensitive action by schools and the Education Welfare Service.' Paragraph 3.10 requires the outcome of the consultation to be confirmed in writing, indicating whether the social services department is involved with the child or the family, and if there are any known reasons why an education supervision order would not be appropriate. The social services department may seek the assistance of the education authority in the provision of services for the child, who are under a duty to comply with the request in accordance with s 27(1)–(3) CA 1989. There is a reciprocal arrangement in s 27(4) which also requires every local authority to assist any local education authority with the provision of services for any child within the local authority's area who has special educational needs.

9.4 Practice and procedure

9.4.1 Application

The applicant is the local education authority. The application should be made on form C17. Applications to renew an order are made on form CI7A. Applications are 'family proceedings' under s 8(3) and (4) CA 1989, and therefore the menu of orders is available to the court (see Figure 8, below, pp 124-25). The principles in s 1 CA 1989 apply, see Chapter 2 above. An application may not be made in respect of a child subject to a care order, s 36(6) CA 1989.

9.4.2 Venue

Cases should be commenced in the Family Proceedings Court, but may be transferred to the county court or the High Court. If the county court or the High Court has directed an investigation of the child's circumstances under s 37(1) CA 1989, the application may be made to that court or a nominated care centre. If there are proceedings pending in a court, then the application may commence there.

9.4.3 Notice

Rule 9(3)(4) Family Proceedings Court (Children Act) 1989 Rules 1991 SI 1991/1395 and r 4.9(3)(4) Family Proceedings Rules 1991 SI 1991/1247 provide that seven days' notice of the hearing or directions appointment must be given, with the date and venue of the application.

A local authority providing accommodation for the child, or the person with whom a child is living, or the manager of a refuge providing accommodation for the child under s 51 CA 1989 may be served with notice of the application, r 4 Family Proceedings Court (Children Act) Rules and r 4.4 Family Proceedings Rules 1991.

9.4.4 Respondents

Every person with parental responsibility for the child is a respondent, as is the child. Respondents should be served with notice of the application, together with a copy of the application in form C17. Respondents may file and serve an answer two days before the hearing.

9.4.5 Service

The normal rules of service apply, see r 4 Family Proceedings Court (Children Act) Rules and r 4.4 Family Proceedings Rules 1991. The court also has power under the rules to vary or waive service.

9.5 Rights of the child

These are:

(a) the child's welfare is paramount;

(b) to be consulted on schooling issues;

(c) to have wishes and feelings taken into consideration;

(d) to be a respondent in the application if of sufficient age and understanding;

(e) to receive directions that are reasonable;

(f) to advice, assistance and befriending from the supervisor.

9.6 Variation, discharge and appeals

Discharge can be on the application of the child, the parents, or the local education authority, para 17(1), Sch 3 CA 1989. The court on discharge may order the local authority to investigate the child's circumstances under s 37 and para 17(2), Sch 3 CA 1989.

The order may be extended for up to three years on application by the authority within three months before the expiry date, and the order can be extended more than once, para 15, Sch 3 CA 1989.

9.6.1 Appeals

Appeals from the family proceedings court now lie to the county court. Orders made in the county court or High Court may be appealed to the Court of Appeal.

Interestingly, the European Convention for the Protection of Human Rights envisages the use of secure accommodation to detain a minor for 'educational supervision', Art 5.

However, read in conjunction with Art 8 (right to family life), it is unlikely that in the UK this would encourage courts to take a step in that direction, but it would be interesting to watch case law as it develops in this area.

10 Police Powers Under the Children Act 1989

Police have special powers under s 46 of the Children Act 1989 (CA 1989) referred to as 'police protection', which do not need a court order. The ground for action is that police have reasonable cause to believe the child would otherwise suffer significant harm, s 46(2).

These powers are:

* to remove a child to a safe place and keep him there, s 46(1)(a);
* to prevent a child's removal from a safe place, s 46(1)(b);
* no power to enter premises without a warrant unless s 17 Police and Criminal Evidence Act 1984 satisfied (s 17 includes saving life and limb, prevention of serious damage to property, or arrests);
* police must safeguard and promote the child's welfare, s 46(9)(b).

The maximum duration for the exercise of s 46 powers is 72 hours, s 46(6).

Each area must have a 'designated police officer' responsible for carrying out the duties imposed by CA 1989, who can apply for emergency protection if necessary, ss 46(3)(e) and 46(7).

The police must, under s 46(3), inform the local authority of their action, the reasons for it, and the child's whereabouts; inform the child and discover his wishes and feelings; remove the child to local authority accommodation and, under s 46(4), take reasonable steps to inform parents, those with parental responsibility, and those with whom the child was living, of the action, the reasons for it, and future plans.

11 Instructions and Case Preparation in Family Proceedings

Family proceedings are non-adversarial. Advocates may be instructed to represent children, parents, other parties, or local authorities; and effective advocacy depends more on thorough preparation of the case, coupled with good negotiation skills with all parties throughout the proceedings than on the final presentation in court.

The first task is to elicit from all sources available as much information as possible about the circumstances of the case, the client, and the child. All evidence relevant to the welfare of the child should be available to the court.

11.1 Action plan on receipt of instructions from an adult or local authority

- Arrange to interview the client or instructing social worker as soon as possible.

- Where appropriate, check the legal aid situation and complete the necessary forms.

- Obtain copies of all applications and documents which have been filed with the court.

- Are there other relevant proceedings current or pending? Obtain details.

- Have there been previous proceedings in relation to the child(ren) or the family?

    If so, ask for copies of all previous/existing court orders and copies of documents filed with the court. Consent and appropriate directions by the court may be necessary to authorise and facilitate disclosure of documents from another court or from other proceedings.

- Ascertain who the other parties are. Check whether they have instructed legal representatives, and obtain details.

- Identify any other people who should be made parties to the proceedings or notified of the proceedings in accordance with the Rules, and take appropriate action.

- Let the court and all other parties (or their advocates if they are represented) and the children's guardian know you are instructed in the matter, and write, inviting communication and offering co-operation.

  (See Chapter 15 if you are instructed by the children's guardian on behalf of the child.)

- Interview potential witnesses.

- Follow the PLO procedures.

11.2 Interviewing clients

Cases involving family breakup or issues of child protection are stressful for all the parties concerned. It is essential to establish a relationship of trust with clients, giving them space in the initial interview to express their feelings, whilst at the same time keeping the interview focused on taking background history and instructions. Set aside sufficient time to allow clients to fully express all they have to say and offer appropriate refreshments – this can provide a welcome break. A checklist may assist to keep the interview focused on the information required. Below are sample checklists of some basic issues to cover when interviewing parents, social workers, and medical witnesses, to which can be added specific issues relevant to each case.

11.2.1 Checklist for information from parents

- Full name Address

- Home telephone number   (Any restrictions on its use?)

- Work telephone number   (Any restrictions on its use?)

- Mobile telephone number (Any restrictions on its use?)

- Names of all the children of the family and their dates of birth.

- Who are the parents of each child of the family?

- Who has parental responsibility for the child?

- Where does each child of the family live, if they do not live with the client?

- What are the present contact arrangements with the children living elsewhere?

- Partner and family members living in client's household Close or significant family members living outside household The family's social/cultural/racial/ religious context

- Does this client, any member of the family, or the child(ren), have any special needs, cultural issues, language problems, etc of which the court, children's guardian and other parties need to be aware?

- Obtain general information about this client, including: background, education, attainments, current or past employment, interests, and significant life events.

- Does this client, or any partner, family member, carer, or co-habitee, have any convictions for offences which may affect an assessment of their capacity to care for the child(ren)? For example, conviction for an offence listed in Sch 1 of the Children and Young Persons Act 1933, drink or drugs related offences, etc?

  Convictions should be disclosed to the court: *Re R (Minors) (Custody)* [1986] 1 FLR 6.

- Does the client or any family member have any particular skills or attributes relevant to their parenting ability?

- Have there been any previous court orders or applications made to a court in respect of this child, or any other child of the family or any family member?

- Other people involved with the family who may be able to assist in providing information:

  (a) schools attended by the child(ren)

  (b) playgroups

  (c) voluntary organisations/religious organisations

  (d) therapists

  (e) GP/hospital

  (f) health visitor

  (g) community, religious or other agencies or organisations involved with the family

  - How does the client see the present situation?

Obtain:

(a) details of the circumstances that led up to this application

(b) a description of the current situation and presenting problems

(c) the client's wishes, feelings and concerns

(d) the client's instructions as to what they wish to happen in this case (subject to the legal advice they may receive now or later).

• Does the client have any comments to make or explanations to offer about causation of any injuries or harm alleged, or the child's emotional problems?

• What contact has the client had to date with social services, or other professionals about this child?

• Has the client requested or received any help, advice, or resources from social services?

• What would the client like to see happen in the future concerning the child(ren)?

• What would the child(ren) like to happen?

• What does the client think that others will say about the situation? (Often a very revealing question)

• Can the client think of others who may be able to offer relevant information about the child or family?

PLO requirements on information from local authorities and social workers

The PLO checklist is now the one that is used to ensure that social workers and local authorities have provided all the information and documentation that is required of them. There are pro formas and checklists to be followed. Annexe A to the PLO has the list of documents to be filed with any application for care or supervision. Annex B sets out the Local Authority's Case Summary. In order to prevent accidental omissions, Annexe C provides a pro forma for a draft case Management Order.

There tends to be a separate chronology prepared for court and social work statements are factual accounts of recent events leading to the application. There is now a letter before action which sets out in clear terms what is considered to be the problem. Most of the information now is contained in the Core Assessment and the PLO provides for the filing of records of discussions with the family and key local authority minutes and records for the child, including strategy discussions. See chapter 7 and (Pressdee et al 2008), for further discussion of the PLO.

Care plan and written agreements should bear in mind the welfare checklist, and the *Children Act 1989 Guidance and Regulations* Vol 3 *Family Placements*, pp 15-16, para 2.62, also *Framework for Assessment and Assessing Children in Need* and LAC 99/29). See, also Chapter 7 (at 7.1.1.-7.1.4) above and below, Chapter 16.

11.2.2   Checklist for basic initial information from medical witnesses

There is guidance in the PLO and *Practice Direction: Experts 2008* as to the content of the letter of instruction to an expert and also the required content of an expert's report. Please refer to Chapter 18 for discussion of the instruction of experts, expert evidence and medical reports. In addition to this, the checklist below indicates the basic information which might be included in the report of a medical witness.

*   Medical Witness's full name

*   Health centre/surgery/hospital address Post held

*   Relevant qualifications and experience

*   Ensure that any opinions expressed are objective, relevant, and supported by observations

*   Nature, extent, venue and duration of examination(s) of the child:

    (a)   date, duration and venue of first examination

    (b)   reason for referral

    (c)   observations of child on examination

    (d)   appearance, demeanour, attitude to examination and others present

    (e)   note any statements made by the child or by others that are relevant

    (f)   any abnormalities in physical or mental state

    (g)   marks, abrasions, wounds, skeletal survey, pain, tenderness

    (h)   unusual features or appearance of any part of the body

- Body map showing location of areas of injury, bruising etc can be very helpful

- Colour photographs are of great help to a court if the child/family is willing to allow this, but beware, if sexual abuse is alleged, photography may remind child of the abuse or be further abusive

- Description of the general health of the child

- Full description of the child's injuries/abnormalities, with an explanation of the medical terms used.

- Is it possible to give a time of the occurrence of any injuries noted?

- When the injuries occurred, would they have caused pain to the child? Would he or she have cried out, screamed in pain? Does it still hurt? How soon afterwards would it stop hurting? Should a caring adult have noticed/treated the child's discomfort/pain?

- Were there attempts to treat the injuries/or to cover them up?

- Is there any evidence of brittle bones or other congenital factor likely to contribute to these injuries or explain them?

- If anyone was questioned about the injuries, note who was questioned, who was present, their reactions and demeanour in response to questioning, specific questions used, and responses given

- Note any comments or explanations offered of how the injuries/abnormalities occurred

- Does any explanation given by adults agree/conflict with the medical or psychiatric diagnosis?

- Describe diagnosis, treatment given or recommended following examination and prognosis

- Note date(s), venue and duration of subsequent examinations

- Record any other relevant or significant health issues within family (including parents, siblings, other relatives), particularly any issues affecting the parents' or carers' ability to look after the child, or affecting the general health and welfare of the child or close family members

- Health history of the child, in chronological order, including:

  (a) physical development

  (b) height/weight/centile charts

  (c) developmental assessments according to age

(d) visual/hearing/neurological/speech/language assessments

(e) evidence of emotional problems/abnormalities (have they been diagnosed as a congenital disorder, or is there possibly some other cause?)

(f) evidence of physical problems/abnormalities. (Do they constitute an illness or 'disability' within the meaning of the Children Act? Have they been diagnosed as a congenital disorder, or is there possibly some other cause?)

(g) treatment(s) given to the child and the the effect of treatment

(h) advice offered to the family/child about medical care and whether the advice was taken up and acted upon

• Up to date information about the child's development

• Other information concerning the child's welfare that is relevant for the helping agencies and the court

Medical witnesses should bear in mind the welfare checklist whilst writing their report. It is a useful reference concerning the best interests of the child shared by the court, the children's guardian and the professionals in the case.

Include the names and addresses of doctors and other health professionals who have been involved with the child/family, or to whom child the child has been referred for specialist treatment or examination. They may be able to give additional relevant information.

Include a list of 'dates to avoid', that is, times when unavailable for court, conferences and meetings.

A report should end with a 'statement of truth' see PLO para 3.3 (13).

11.3 Preparation of the case

Good advocacy is not just an ability to speak persuasively in court. It is mostly good preparation. A good grasp of the facts of the case, the issues and the relevant law will generate confidence when putting forward an argument or making a point. Research on an issue will assist an advocate to ask questions that are useful to the court.. Effective child and family law advocates are non-adversarial in approach, willing to negotiate, and when in court, they are courteous, clear, concise and accurate, having read all the case documentation thoroughly before the hearing.

A sound knowledge of the relevant law and the rules of evidence and procedure is essential and it is also vitally important to keep up to date with changes. For essential reading and sources for wider reference, see Chapter 19.

Recently, the Law Society warned practitioners about placing reliance on the internet for legal information. Many blogs and unofficial websites offer legal information, but their accuracy relies upon the expertise of the writers, and may be questionable. Visit the government and official websites, and always go to the original source for case law, statute and subsidiary legislation. The UK government website, www. statutelaw.gov.uk/, provides updated statutes, tracking changes as they are made. Other useful websites are listed at the end of this book.

11.4 Burden of proof in child law cases

Generally, the person alleging a fact must prove it. In child protection, the burden of proof is on a balance of probability, that is 'it is more likely than not' that there is actual or a potential risk of significant harm to the child. Neither the seriousness of any allegations nor the seriousness of the consequences should make any difference to the standard of proof to be applied in determining the facts. See the House of Lords case of *Re B (Children) (Care orders: Standard of Proof)* (2008) Times Law Reports 12 June 2008. We will have to await the full impact of the judgment in future cases.

As *Children Law & Practice* (Hershman and McFarlane) points out at C-92, the balance of probability means may be taken to mean a more than 50% chance, but when considering the 'likelihood' of suffering significant harm as a future possibility, the House of Lords put it very clearly as '…a real possibility, a possibility that cannot be sensibly ignored, having regard to the nature and gravity of the feared harm in the particular case …' For the full judgment see *Re H and others (Child Sexual Abuse: Standard of Proof)* [1996] 1 All ER 1; [1996] 1FLR 80, discussed earlier in Chapter 7 at 7.3.1.

11.5 Special evidence rules in child law cases

Child law cases should be non-adversarial. The focus of the case is the welfare of the child. The rules of evidence in child protection differ from other areas of law. The Children Act encourages admission of actions affecting the child without these becoming the basis for prosecution. In wardship proceedings the strict rules of evidence do not apply, see Butler-Sloss LJ in *Re H (Minor), Re K (Minors) (Child abuse: Evidence)* [1989] 2 FLR 313, pp 332-33. The general rules of evidence in non-child law cases render certain evidence inadmissible, that is, that relating to character, hearsay and opinion. In child law cases this evidence is admissible, see Figure 4.

11.5.1 Character

In child law cases, consideration of the character of those who care for the child is vitally important and evidence of convictions, medical and psychiatric history are admissible.

11.5.2 Best evidence and hearsay

The hearsay rule provides that witnesses may only give an account of what they themselves actually experienced as evidence of the truth of the alleged event. If a witness tells the court what someone else said, the words quoted cannot be admitted as proof that the thing reported actually happened. If A tells the court that 'On 14 July 2000, B said, "C hit me"', under the hearsay rule, this statement proves only that on that day B was alive and able to speak; that B spoke to A and that A heard his words; but it is not sufficient to prove that C did in fact hit B. B personally would have to come and give evidence of the event.

In child law cases, however, the court requires all relevant evidence, and in certain circumstances, it admits hearsay. The wishes and feelings of children are important, and quotations from others about the child or of what the child said can be vital. Section 96(3) CA 1989, and the Children (Admissibility of Hearsay Evidence) Order 1993 ST 1993/621 provide that in civil proceedings before the High Court or a county court, family proceedings, and civil proceedings in a magistrates' court under the Child Support Act 1991, evidence given in connection with the upbringing, maintenance or welfare of a child, shall be admissible notwithstanding any rule of law relating to hearsay. Family proceedings are defined in ss 8(3) and 105 CA 1989. Refer to s 4 of the Civil Evidence Act 1995 for helpful criteria in assessment of hearsay evidence.

The court requires the originals of all notes produced, that includes those made contemporaneously, not just the neatly typed copies made later on. Notes should be written up at the time or as soon as possible after the event recorded. If notes are made days after an event, their reliability may be questioned.

11.5.3 Opinion

Witnesses may give factual or expert evidence. Witnesses of fact may not give their opinion and are expected to restrict themselves to a full and accurate account of what happened. The court draws inferences from the facts. Experts may draw inferences, and offer opinions based on the facts, research and their own learning and experience. They should behave in a professional manner, and be impartial, see Chapter 18.

11.5.4 Statements made by children's guardians

Under s 41(11) (a)–(b) CA 1989, the court may take account of any statement contained in the report of a children's guardian, and of any evidence given in respect of matters referred to in the guardian's report. The court has the power to regulate its own proceedings, and will assess the weight to give to such evidence. The children's guardian has access to (and may cite) local authority records, see s 42 CA 1989; and should draw to the attention of the court for directions any local authority papers which are relevant, but which the local authority does not intend to disclose, see *Re C (Expert Evidence: Disclosure: Practice)* [1995] 1 FLR 204.

11.5.5 No professional privilege for medical or psychiatric reports

Medical records must be disclosed on production of a *subpoena duces tecum* issued with leave of a District Judge. *Practice Direction (Family Proceedings: Case Management)* [1995] 1 FLR 456 requires full and frank disclosure of material in all matters relating to children, because the welfare of the child is of paramount importance. This includes medical reports unfavourable to a client's interests, see *Essex CC v R (A Minor)* [1993] 2 FLR 826, and *Oxfordshire CC v M* [1994] 1 FLR 175, in which the Court of Appeal upheld this principle. Communications between lawyer and client remain privileged.

11.5.6 Directions hearings – ordering the evidence

Delay must be avoided, s 1(3) CA 1989. Directions appointments enable the court to control the preparation of evidence and listing hearings. The Children Act Advisory Committee has produced a useful pro forma for standard directions for both public and private family law proceedings.

Leave of the court is required for disclosure of documents to experts or to other non parties; to withhold evidence from a party; and for medical or psychiatric examinations or assessments of children. Where one party seeks to prevent another from seeing a document, an application should be made on notice and transferred to the High Court (*Re M (Disclosure)* [1998] 2 FLR 1028). The directions may also

Figure 4: Admissible evidence in care proceedings

ORAL EVIDENCE may be given by:		ANY WITNESS MAY PRODUCE ALL OR ANY OF THESE:	
The child ...	Provided that the court is satisfied on enquiry that they understand the duty to tell the truth.	Photographs	Provided produced by taker, who has unretouched negatives and can produce originals.
Any witness of fact	Hearsay rule not applicable in family proceedings. Witness may not give opinions.	Tape recordings	Provided shown to be original and not tampered with.
An expert withness	May give fact and opinion, can refer to charts, notes, tables and reference works.	X-rays	As photographs.
		Other objects	eg clothing, weapons, admissible provided relevant.
		Video recordings	If of an incident, admissible as photograph. Admissibility and content of interviews may be questioned.

Notes may be used provided that they were made contemporaneously with events, or sufficiently soon thereafter for the memory of the person making the note to be clear.

DOCUMENTARY EVIDENCE:

May be admissible provided it complies with s 1 Evidence Act 1938. Personal knowledge of facts/or statement of fact is or forms part of continuous record in which the maker recorded facts given by another who had personal knowledge of them and maker gives evidence. Medical notes come into this category. Special rules for computer records. Copies may be accepted for same reason if certified to be true copies. Documents copied by the children's guardian may be adduced in evidence, s 42 CA 1989.

SELF-PRODUCING DOCUMENTS:

Memorandum of conviction	Admissible under s 7(2) of the Rehabilitation of Offenders Act 1974, Sched 13 of the Children Act 1989, and s 73 of the Polic and Criminal Evidence Act 1984, and Home Office Circulars 88/1982; 105/1982; and 102/1988, and see Police Act 1997, Pt V.
School attendance records	Admissible under s 95 Education Act 1944.
Medical certificate	Admissible under s 26 CYPA 1963.

stipulate the venue of any assessments to be carried out, who should accompany the child and to whom the results should be given. See also *Re X (Disclosure for the purposes of ciminal proceedings)* [2008] EWHC 242 (Fam); [2008] Fam Law 725 and *Re M (Case disclosure to police)* Baron J [2008] Fam Law 618.

Before the directions hearing the advocate should ascertain whether experts are available, how long assessments will take, cost, legal aid and any assistance the experts may require. The expert should confirm availability, enabling the court to fix a suitable hearing date.

11.6 Court procedure at the hearing

Procedure is addressed separately in the chapters dealing with each order. However, hearings follow a reasonably consistent pattern common to most Children Act applications.

11.6.1 Notes of evidence

There is a duty on the court to take a note of the 'substance of oral evidence given' at the proceedings, r 20 Family Proceedings (Children Act 1989) Rules 1991 and r 4.20 Family Proceedings Rules 1991.

11.6.2 Order of evidence

Rule 21(2) Family Proceedings (Children Act 1989) Rules 1991 and Rule 4.21(2) Family Proceedings Rules 1991 empower the court to regulate its own proceedings, for example, vary the order of speeches and evidence to suit the needs of the case and the people involved.

Unless the courts create a variation of procedure, r 21(3) and r 4.21(3) respectively set out the order of evidence as follows:

(a) applicant;

(b) any party with parental responsibility for the child;

(c) other respondents (including a child who is separately represented);

(d) the children's guardian;

(e) the child, if he is not a party and there is no children's guardian.

(This is a situation mainly relevant to private law cases, since in most Pt IV CA 1989 cases there is a children's guardian appointed and a child of sufficient age to instruct a lawyer separately will be a party.)

11.6.3 Extent of evidence

There are some limitations on the courts regulating their own proceedings. They must hear some evidence, even if the matter is agreed. It is not normally sufficient to file statements and to rely on these to support a case, calling no oral evidence at all, although this may occur in exceptional circumstances. In *Re B (Minors) (Contact)* [1994] 2 FLR 1, Butler-Sloss LJ in the Court of Appeal, hearing an issue of defined contact, gave guidance to the courts on approaching the matter of how much evidence is appropriate, p 6A(1)–(6).

In *Re F (Minor) (Care Order: Procedure)* [1994] 1 FLR 240 a magistrates' court which had heard evidence from the local authority but refused to hear the evidence of the father was held to be quite wrong. The justices should have heard the evidence from both sides. In *S v Merton LBC* [1994] 1 FCR 186, a family proceedings court was criticised for making its decision on submissions only and it was held that some evidence at least is required! See Munby J on bundles in *Re X and Y (Court Bundles)* [2008] EWHC 2058 (Fam).

11.6.4 Directions hearing checklist

List of witnesses

Dates to avoid

- parties
- witnesses of fact
- expert witnesses
- advocate's engagements

Information and assistance for court proceedings

- reference material
- exhibits
- interpreter
- visual aids in court
- TV links; tape recorder/player
- security
- wheelchair access
- hearing loop, etc

Information for expert witnesses

- documents in case (leave required for disclosure to expert)
- exhibits to be sent to expert or in expert's possession
- chronology
- arrangements for conference of experts

Leave of the court or consents necessary

- disclosure of documents, information, exhibits
- medical or psychiatric examinations and their venue, who will accompany child, to whom results are to be given
- bloods or other special testing (does it need High Court consent, for example HIV?)
- excuse party/child attendance at court
- accommodation of child
- withholding information from party (High Court consent)

Statements and reports to be filed with the court

- parties; witnesses; experts; chronology; reports; other
- documents from files

Statements or reports late?

- consent of the court required for late filing

Service

- applicant and parties; those entitled to notice of the proceedings; those entitled to be respondents; children's guardian; others

11.7 Courtroom skills

11.7.1 Court manners

Proceedings are non-adversarial, and in an inevitably emotional situation, a calm advocate can assist everyone greatly in family proceedings. Forms of address are as follows:

Magistrates	Your Worship, Sir or Madam (usually pronounced Ma'am)
Deputy/District Judge	Sir or Madam (pronounced Ma'am)
County Court Judge	Your Honour

Figure 5: Layout of typical family proceedings court

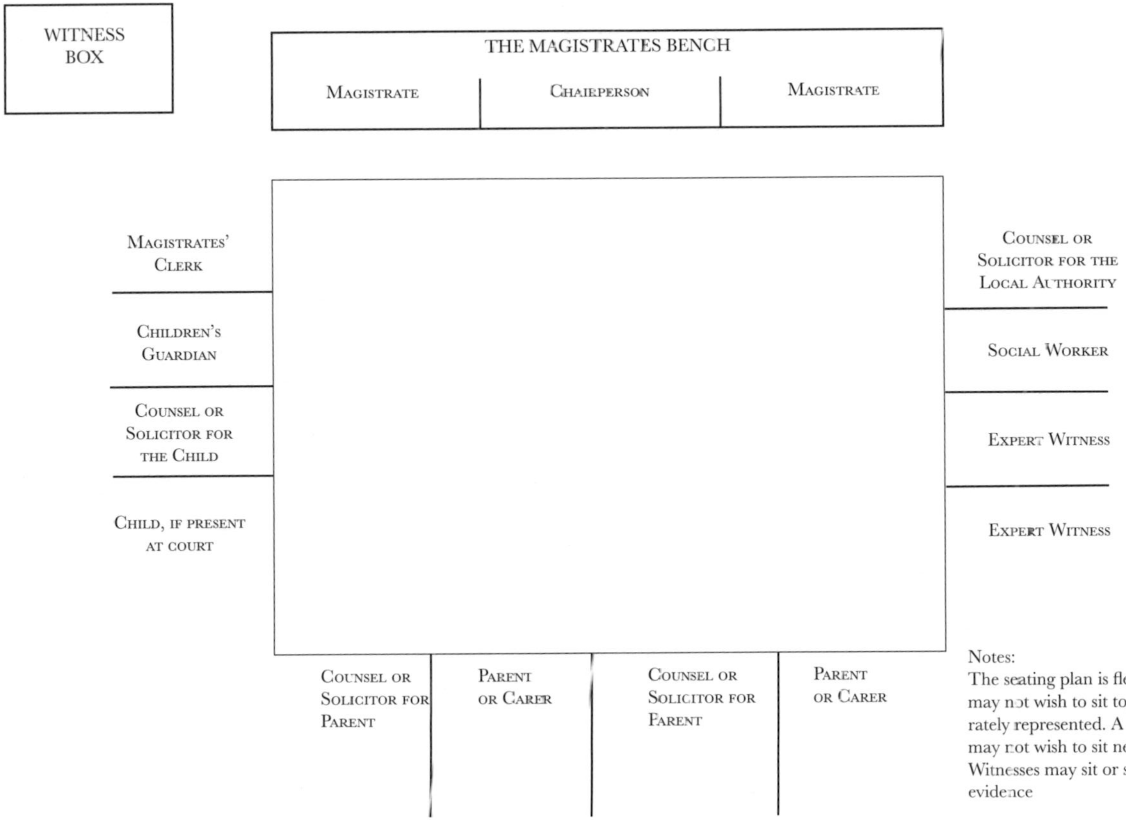

WITNESS BOX	

THE MAGISTRATES BENCH		
MAGISTRATE	CHAIRPERSON	MAGISTRATE

MAGISTRATES' CLERK

CHILDREN'S GUARDIAN

COUNSEL OR SOLICITOR FOR THE CHILD

CHILD, IF PRESENT AT COURT

COUNSEL OR SOLICITOR FOR THE LOCAL AUTHORITY

SOCIAL WORKER

EXPERT WITNESS

EXPERT WITNESS

COUNSEL OR SOLICITOR FOR PARENT

PARENT OR CARER

COUNSEL OR SOLICITOR FOR PARENT

PARENT OR CARER

Notes:
The seating plan is flexible. Parents may not wish to sit together if separately represented. A child, if present, may not wish to sit next to parents. Witnesses may sit or stand to give evidence

High Court and Court of Appeal Judges	My Lord or My Lady (often pronounced by the Bar as M'Lud or M'Lady)
Barristers and solicitors referring to each other	My (learned) friend, Counsel for X or Mr, Mrs or Ms ... etc

Cases are listed on a notice outside the court room with the time of hearing. Children cases are often listed just by the court reference number or otherwise anonymised, e.g. *Kent County Council v X*. Greet other parties and advocates on arrival at court, letting the court usher know of your arrival. Ushers enter the names of everyone present on their court list.

In court, stand while the judge or magistrates enter the room, and allow them to sit before sitting yourself. Figure 5, above, illustrates a typical family proceedings courtroom layout and seating. The family proceedings courts and county courts may conduct their proceedings seated. Check with the clerk to the court. The general rule for advocates or witnesses is to stand until invited to sit.

The applicant's advocate usually introduces other advocates and the parties to the court, or the judge or magistrate may invite people to introduce themselves, so, to be prepared, find out the names of others before going in.

The task of an advocate is to present the facts and the law to the court and to put forward to the court their client's point of view in a reasoned and courteous manner. In children cases, questioning should be to elicit clarity and detail, and not be adversarial. Advocates will therefore be asking questions of witnesses to clarify statements filed with the court or to elicit new information. If asking a question to which you do not know the answer, be prepared for surprises!

Do not interrupt another advocate or witness when they are addressing the court. Allow them to finish what they were saying, then request the court's permission to correct any factual or legal errors. Don't interrupt the advocate who is asking questions, wait, let them finish, then speak. Advise witnesses to turn slightly to face the bench, and maintain eye contact with the judge or the magistrates whilst addressing all answers to them (rather than to the advocate asking questions). This is not only good court practice, but it also very effectively prevents advocates from interrupting, as to do so would then seem discourteous to the judge or magistrates. If an over enthusiastic or aggressive advocate does interrupt before a witness has said all that they wanted to, advise them to simply turn to the judge or bench and say, politely, that before they answer that new question, they would like to finish the point that they wanted to make in response to the earlier one, and then do so.

Making audible comments or critical 'asides' in court to other advocates or clients is not acceptable, and is unprofessional.

Bring to court sufficient spare copies of documents and draft orders for all the parties who need to have one. The original goes to the judge or bench, with a copy to the clerk. If there are magistrates, each should have a copy if possible.

The examination of witnesses follows the order of evidence (see above). Each witness is called to the witness box by the party calling him, sworn in or requested to affirm and then examined in chief. Questions which suggest an answer are 'leading questions' and forbidden in examination in chief; one must not 'lead the witness'. For example, ask 'What time of day was it when…?' not 'Was it three o'clock when…?'

The other parties may then cross-examine the witness. Finally, the party calling the witness may re-examine to clarify points already made. The court should then be offered the opportunity to ask questions of the witness. Ask permission before the witness leaves the court, if not required further.

Traditionally, the applicant opens the case and outlines their case to the court. The other parties then have the opportunity to make a speech to the court but they will usually do so at the end of the case. The children's guardian or the child's advocate will be the last to speak. If there are submissions on law during the case, the order of address follows the order of evidence.

When the case is completed, stand for the magistrates or judge to leave the room.

These notes are necessarily brief, but there are many good books and courses on advocacy, and by far the best way of learning courtroom skills is to sit in on cases with experienced Children Panel advocates – not necessarily to copy their style, but to learn by observation. In this way, we can all develop our own individual strengths and skills as advocates, or become efficient and cogent professional witnesses.

12 Children's Rights

The law affecting the rights of children includes: the Children Act 1989 (CA 1989); the UN Convention on the Rights of the Child (in force in the UK on 15 January 1992); the Human Rights Act 1998 (in force in the UK from 2 October 2000); and the European Convention for the Protection of Human Rights and Fundamental Freedoms (ECHR) and its Protocols. Other legislation affords specific rights to children and families, for example Mental Health and is cited below where relevant.

Under s 22(4) of the Human Rights Act 1998, all proceedings brought by a public authority are subject to the ECHR, even where the alleged breach of these rights occurred before the coming into force of the Human Rights Act.

It is important to make a clear distinction between two situations in which consent may be required. The first is where doctors seek to carry out diagnostic assessments which may be necessary before deciding on the best method of treatment, and/or medical, psychiatric, or psychological treatments necessary to maintain the child's health and welfare.

The second category is where medical, psychiatric or psychological assessments are sought for purely forensic purposes.

Depending on the child's age and other considerations, in special circumstances the courts may overrule a child's refusal of necessary treatment, but the courts will be far less willing to overrule a child's refusal of an assessment for forensic purposes.

12.1 To accept or refuse medical treatment

No adult or child competent to make their own medical decisions may be given medical treatment without their consent. Treatment without consent (save in emergencies) may incur liability for damages for assault, or constitute an offence in criminal law. Detention in hospital or any other place without consent could constitute false imprisonment.

The issue, therefore, is at what age can a child give valid consent?

12.1.1 Children over the age of 16 (but under 18)

Under s 8 of the Family Law Reform Act 1969, at the age of 16, a young person gains the right to give informed consent to surgical, medical or dental treatment. Examinations or assessments must impliedly be included. The consent of the young person is as valid as that of an adult. A young person with mental illness, disability, or psychiatric disturbance is subject to the Mental Health Acts.

If a young person consents to recommended medical or dental treatment, therefore, (even if their parents disagreed for some reason) the medical or dental practitioner would be protected from a claim for damages for trespass to the person.

However, if the young person refuses recommended treatment, although those with parental responsibility for the young person may give a valid consent which will have the effect of protecting the medical or dental practitioner from claims for damages for trespass to the person; it should be noted that as the age of the young person increases towards 18, their refusal and the reasons for it are important considerations for parents and the court.

In the event of a dispute about consent for medical treatment, the issue should be taken before the High Court, either under its inherent jurisdiction or under s 8 CA 1989 for a specific issue order. In the case of *Re W (A Minor) (Consent to Medical Treatment)* [1993] 1 FLR 1 the Court of Appeal gave consent for the treatment of a girl of 16 with anorexia nervosa, despite her refusal.

In circumstances requiring sterilisation; termination of a pregnancy; or surgical interventions to save or prolong the child's life, if the child is a ward of court, the High Court's consent is required.

If parents refuse to allow medical treatment and a child needs it, the High Court can provide the requisite authority under its inherent jurisdiction.

12.1.2 Children under 16

The legal situation for consent by children under 16 but who are judged to be '*Gillick* competent' is similar to that of young people over 16, described in 12.1.1 above. For those who are not considered to be '*Gillick* competent', decisions concerning medical treatment are made for them by those with parental responsibility and, where necessary, the courts will intervene or assist in the ways described above.

In *Gillick v West Norfolk and Wisbech AHA* [1986] AC 112 the House of Lords formulated the concept now known colloquially as '*Gillick* competence' in which the ability of a child under 16 to make her own medical decisions is evaluated according to chronological age considered in conjunction with the child's mental and emotional maturity, intelligence and comprehension.

Lord Scarman said:

> It will be a question of fact whether a child seeking advice has sufficient understanding of what is involved to give a consent valid in law. Until the child achieves the capacity to consent, the parental right to make the decision continues save only in exceptional circumstances. Emergency, parental neglect, abandonment of the child, or inability to find the parent are examples of exceptional situations

'*Gillick* competence' has been reviewed in a number of subsequent cases. The most notable recent case was *R (Axon) v Secrretary of State for Health* [2006] EWHC Admin 37 1QB, in which a mother challenged through judicial review the Department of Health guidance for confidentiality on the issue of the provision of abortion for her daughter aged 15, without her mother's knowledge. The court held that the *Gillick* decision remained authoritative as to the lawfulness of the provision by health care professionals of confidential advice and treatment to young people under 16, without parental knowledge or consent. The *Gillick* guidelines must, however, be strictly observed.

In *Re S (Minor) (Refusal of Treatment)* [1995] 1 FCR 604 it was held that a girl of almost 16 suffering from thalassaemia major should continue with her treatment, despite her refusal to do so on religious grounds. The discontinuance of treatment would have resulted in her death within a few weeks. The court acknowledged that at 18 she could refuse and effectively end her life, but expressed the hope that in the intervening period she might change her mind, or that gene therapy would relieve her condition.

See also *Re L (Medical Treatment: Gillick Competency)* [1998] 2 FLR 810, and *Re M (Child:Refusal of Medical Treatment)* [1999] 2 FCR 577, where a heart transplant was authorised for a 15 year old girl.

Understanding the potential consequences of refusing treatment or assessment increases with age and maturity, and the child's intelligence and level of understanding, influenced by the detail of the information provided. *The National Health Service Guide to Consent for Examination or Treatment* (1990) HC (90) 22 recommends that doctors should record factual information given to the child, including questions asked and the child's responses, for possible reference later if the child's ability to make the decision were to be questioned. Where a child is seen alone, efforts should be made to obtain the child's agreement to inform their parents, save where this is clearly not in the child's best interests.

For medical and psychiatric treatment in the context of supervision orders, see below, 12.2.1.

12.1.3 Mentally disordered children

Where a child is mentally ill or mentally disordered and unable to make a legally valid decision for himself, the High Court in its wardship jurisdiction may consent on behalf of a person under 18. The High Court may order reasonable force to be used to ensure compliance, see *A Metropolitan Borough Council v DB* [1997] 1 FLR 767.

12.1.4 Where nobody has parental responsibility

In situations where an immediate decision or action is needed and no one with parental responsibility is available, s 3(5) CA 1989 provides:

> a person who:
>
> (a) does not have parental responsibility for a particular child; but
>
> (b) has care of the child,
>
> may ... do what is reasonable in all the circumstances of the case for the purpose of safeguarding or promoting the child's welfare.

This section was intended for use by neighbours, relatives, or others looking after children who may need to take the child urgently to the GP or dentist, but should not be used to give consent for major medical decisions.

12.2 To accept or refuse medical or psychiatric assessment

Child protection often necessitates medical or psychiatric examination or assessment. *The Report of the Inquiry into Child Abuse in Cleveland* (1987) demonstrated that repeated medical examinations can themselves be abusive. The court has wide power to set limits by directions, for example, the place and time of an examination; person(s) to be present; person(s) to conduct the examination; and person(s) or authorities to whom the results shall be given.

12.2.1 Circumstances in which the court may direct medical or psychiatric examination or assessment which the child has a right to refuse

In the following circumstances, a child of sufficient understanding has the right to refuse consent to medical or psychiatric examination:

(a) interim care order, s 38(6) CA 1989;

(b) interim supervision order, s 38(6) CA 1989;

(c) emergency protection order, s 44(6)(b) and (7) CA 1989;

(d) child assessment order, s 43(8) CA 1989.

In supervision orders, the child may be directed to undergo a medical, but not a psychiatric examination, but (where the child has sufficient understanding to exercise their right of consent) the court may only make this direction if the child consents, see para 4, Sch 3 CA 1989. The court may order psychiatric or medical treatment of a child under a supervision order in specified circumstances and consent is required of a child who has sufficient understanding to exercise their right of consent, see para 5, Sch 3 CA 1989.

Where the child has the right to refuse medical or psychiatric examinations, his wishes and feelings must be ascertained by the children's guardian, or doctor, see *CA 1989 Guidance and Regulations*, Vol 1, *Court Orders*.

Doctors must check whether the child is capable of giving an informed decision, and that he consents, before proceeding with an examination. Even if the court has directed an examination with the child's consent, if, when the child is with the doctor he then refuses, the doctor should not proceed, but should refer the matter back to the court. If the court agrees that this is an informed decision, then usually the court will respect the refusal, but if the refusal may place the child in serious danger, then it is possible that the High Court may overrule the refusal in the child's best interests. Such an event would be rare.

12.3 To make his or her own application to the court

Under s 10(8) CA 1989, children of sufficient age and understanding may make their own applications for s 8 orders, with leave of the court. Note that all applications by a child for leave to seek a s 8 order should be heard in the High Court – *Practice Direction* [1993] 1 All ER 820; [1993] 1 FLR 668.

Following *Re SC (Minor) (Leave to Seek Residence Order)* [1994] 1 FLR 96, where the child is the applicant, then his welfare is paramount, because the provisions of s 10(9) Children Act 1989 do not apply. (Section 10(9) CA 1989 sets out the criteria for the court's consideration in granting leave for all other applicants, and it has been held that the child's welfare is not paramount in those applications.) Also, everyone with parental responsibility for the child should have notice of the application (see 13.2.2 below).

Children may seek other orders under CA 1989, with leave, including discharge of:

- care;
- supervision;
- emergency protection;
- s 8 orders;
- parental responsibility orders;
- parental responsibility agreements.

The decision as to whether a child is of sufficient age and understanding to apply is a matter initially for the solicitor instructed by the child, but ultimately for the court to decide *Re CT (Minor) (Wardship: Representation)* [1993] 3 WLR 602; [1993] 2 FLR 278. The court could appoint a next friend for the child, usually the Official Solicitor, under rr 9.2A(10)(b) and 9(5) Family Proceedings Rules 1991.

12.4 To request confidentiality and, in the event of disagreement with the children's guardian, to instruct a solicitor separately

Where children are subject to care or supervision applications, the child has a solicitor appointed for them by the children's guardian or the court. The child's solicitor takes instructions from the children's guardian and from the child. A child of sufficient age and understanding may request client confidentiality with their solicitor on specific issues, or generally.

A child of sufficient age and understanding may disagree with the recommendations of the children's guardian, remaining a party with his own solicitor. The guardian will notify the court and continue unrepresented, or appoint another solicitor. Procedure is governed by rr 11(3), 12(1)(a), and 12(3)–(5) Family Proceedings (Children Act 1989) Rules; and rr 4.11(3), 4.12(1)(a), and 4.12(3)-(5) Family Proceedings Rules 1991. The ethics, duties and responsibilities of the solicitor for the child are discussed in Chapter 16 below.

12.5 Rights of a child in care

A child in care has rights protected by Children Act 1989 (CA 1989), the Children Act 2004 (CA 2004), and also by the Guidance issued under them. The child has a right to:

- refuse medical or psychiatric assessment ordered within an interim care order under s 38(6) CA 1989;

- refuse medical or psychiatric assessment in specified circumstances, see above, 12.2;

- reasonable contact with his family, see above, 7.6.4. and paras 9 and 13-16 of *The Care of Children, Principles and Practice in Regulations and Guidance* (1991, London: HMSO) ('*Principles and Practice*');

- be consulted on issues involving her care, see paras 2.21 and 6.4, *Guidance and Regulations* Vol 3; also paras 2.21, 2.45, *Guidance and Regulations* Vol 4, ss 22(4), 61 and 64 CA 1989 and para 25, *Principles and Practice*;

- have his race, culture, religion and background taken into account in care proceedings, s 1 CA 1989 and para 4, *Principles and Practice*;

- consult a solicitor of her own if of sufficient age and understanding, see above, 12.4;

- develop a sense of identity, para 19, *Principles and Practice*;

- grow to independence, para 26, *Principles and Practice*;

- to live in peace and safety, free from abuse, para 3, *Principles and Practice* and Art 3, ECHR;

- regular reviews of his care plan and involvement in the planning in a way appropriate to his age and understanding, paras 3.8, 3.11(a), 3.15, *Guidance and Regulations* Vol 4;

- the child's wishes should also be taken into account when planning for placements and for future care, para 3.20, also ss 22(4), 61 and 64 CA 1989 and para 25, *Principles and Practice*;

- the right to 'family life', Art 8, ECHR, relevant to contact;

- the right to liberty and security, Art 5, ECHR;

- the right not to be treated in an inhuman and degrading way, Art 6, ECHR;

- the right to a 'fair trial', Art 6, ECHR – relevant to forensic evidence, conduct of hearings, admission of evidence. This right could extend to exclusion of a child from a decision making by local authorities and others;

- the rights conferred on children under 18 years in the UN Convention on the Rights of the Child.

13 Other Orders Available to the Court in Family Proceedings

The Children Act 1989 (CA 1989) empowers the court to make certain orders of its own volition in 'family proceedings', defined in s 8(3) and s 105 CA 1989 as amended by subsequent legislation. There is a 'menu' of orders available in family proceedings (see below, Figure 6) from which the court may choose, subject to the principles of s 1 CA 1989. Note that the court should make no order unless it is necessary for the welfare of the child, see Chapter 2. The court cannot, however, intervene in family proceedings to impose orders for care, supervision, secure accommodation, emergency protection or child assessment.

13.1 Orders in family proceedings

Family proceedings, and the 'menu' of orders available, are shown in Figure 6. Family Assistance Orders require no application, but the parties must agree to their making. Special Guardianship Orders may be made of the court's own volition, but require the consent of the person in whose favour it is made, see Chapter 10. Note also that in the magistrates court, unlike the other courts, all proceedings under CA 1989 are classed as family proceedings under s 92(2) CA 1989. Save in the magistrates court, the following orders under CA 1989 are not classed as family proceedings: emergency protection order, child assessment order and recovery orders.

13.2 Section 8 orders

Section 8(1) CA 1989 creates the s 8 orders: contact, prohibited steps, residence and specific issue, all available in all family proceedings. The court may regulate, on an application or of its own volition, the child's residence and contact with others; prohibit specified steps without leave of the court; and deal with any specific issues arising in the child's upbringing.

Figure 6: Family Proceedings and the Menu of Orders available in them

THE PROCEEDINGS SET OUT AROUND THE BOX ARE 'FAMILY PROCEEDINGS' AS DEFINED IN S 8 (4) CA 1989

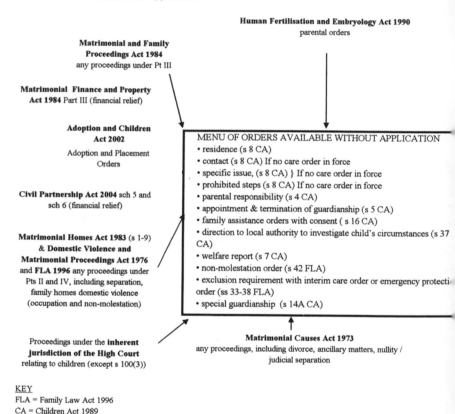

Human Fertilisation and Embryology Act 1990
parental orders

Matrimonial and Family Proceedings Act 1984
any proceedings under Pt III

Matrimonial Finance and Property Act 1984 Part III (financial relief)

Adoption and Children Act 2002
Adoption and Placement Orders

Civil Partnership Act 2004 sch 5 and sch 6 (financial relief)

Matrimonial Homes Act 1983 (s 1-9) **& Domestic Violence and Matrimonial Proceedings Act 1976** and **FLA 1996** any proceedings under Pts II and IV, including separation, family homes domestic violence (occupation and non-molestation)

Proceedings under the **inherent jurisdiction of the High Court** relating to children (except s 100(3))

MENU OF ORDERS AVAILABLE WITHOUT APPLICATION
• residence (s 8 CA)
• contact (s 8 CA) If no care order in force
• specific issue, (s 8 CA) } If no care order in force
• prohibited steps (s 8 CA) If no care order in force
• parental responsibility (s 4 CA)
• appointment & termination of guardianship (s 5 CA)
• family assistance orders with consent (s 16 CA)
• direction to local authority to investigate child's circumstances (s 37 CA)
• welfare report (s 7 CA)
• non-molestation order (s 42 FLA)
• exclusion requirement with interim care order or emergency protecti order (ss 33-38 FLA)
• special guardianship (s 14A CA)

Matrimonial Causes Act 1973
any proceedings, including divorce, ancillary matters, nullity / judicial separation

KEY
FLA = Family Law Act 1996
CA = Children Act 1989
CDA = Crime and Disorder Act 1998

Part II Children Act 1989
s 8 orders:
contact
prohibited steps
residence
specific issue
change of surname (s 13 CA)
removal from jurisdiction (s 13 CA)
family assistance orders (s 16 CA)
financial relief (s 15 CA)
special guardianship (s 14 CA)

Crime And Disorder Act 1998
Proceedings under ss 11 and 12 for
safety orders

MENU OF ORDERS AVAILABLE ONLY ON APPLICATION
application by father or step-father for parental responsibility (s 4 CA)
termination of parental responsibility (s 4 CA)
financial provision (s 15 CA)
care or supervision order (s 31 CA)
education supervision order (s 36 CA)
child assessment order (s 43 CA)
emergency protection order (s 44 CA)
recovery order (s 50 CA)
child safety order (ss 11-12 CDA)
occupation order (ss 33-38 FLA)
residence order (if care order in force)
non-molestation order (s 42 FLA)

Children Act 1989
all cases in the magistrate's courts (s 92
(2) CA)

Emergency protection, child assessment, recovery and
secure accommodation proceedings are not 'family proceedings' under s 8 (4) CA; but ALL cases int he family
proceedings court are included in s 8 (4) CA 1989

Part I Children Act 1989 parental
responsibilty (s -4) guardianship (ss 5
and 6 CA)

Part IV Children Act 1989
care (s 31)
supervision (s 35)
care contact orders (s 34)
education supervision order (s 36)

**Domestic Proceedings,
Magistrate's Courts Act 1978**
maintenance of partners and
children

Some applicants are entitled to apply, and others must first seek the leave of the court. The following are entitled under s 10 CA 1989 to apply for any s 8 order:

(a) any parent or guardian of a child, s 10(4)(a) (this will include the unmarried father of a child whether or not he has parental responsibility);

(b) any person in whose favour a residence order is in force with respect to the child, s 10(4)(b).

The following are entitled to apply for a residence or contact order (but not a prohibited steps order or a specific issue order):

(a) any party to a marriage (whether or not subsisting) in relation to whom the child is a child of the family, s 10(5)(a) (this provision enables a stepparent to seek a residence or contact order);

(b) any person with whom the child has lived for a period of at least three years, s 10(5)(b) (s 10(10) provides that the three year period need not be continuous but must have begun not more than five years before, or ended more than three months before, the making of the application);

(c)   (i) any person who, where there is a residence order in force with respect to the child, has the consent of each of the persons in whose favour the order is made, s 10(5)(c)(i);

(ii) any person who, where there is a care order in force, has the consent of the local authority, s 10(5)(c)(ii) (but note, the court can only make a residence order in such circumstances);

(ii) any person who, in any other case, has the consent of each of those (if any) with parental responsibility for the child, s 10(5)(c)(iii).

13.2.1 Leave to apply

Any other person needs leave to apply for a s 8 order, including the child. The court must be satisfied that a child applicant has sufficient understanding to make the proposed application, and the application must be made to the High Court, see *Practice Direction* [1993] 1 All ER 820. The Court of Appeal has said that this is a 'serious step' which should not be taken lightly. An application by a child in statutory care for a residence order, if successful, would have the effect of discharging the care order.

Note that in *Re A (Care: Discharge Application by a Child)* [1995] 1 FLR 599 Thorpe J held that a child's application to discharge care was not one which required leave of the court.

13.2.2 Considerations on application for leave

Section 10(9) requires that on applications for leave the court should have regard to various considerations which do not include the paramountcy principle. On the issue of leave, the welfare of the child is not of paramount importance because an application for leave is not a trial of the substantive issue, see *North Yorkshire CC v G* [1993] 2 FLR 732. If, however, the child is the applicant, then s 10(9) does not apply, see *Re C (Minor) (Leave to Seek s 8 Order)* [1994] 1 FLR 96.

Section 10(9) sets out the matters to be taken into account:

(a) the nature of the proposed application;

(b) the applicant's connection with the child;

(c) any risk that there might be of that proposed application disrupting the child's life to such an extent that he would be harmed by it; and

(d) where the child is being looked after by a local authority:

    (i) the authority's plans for the child's future; and

    (ii) the wishes and feelings of the child's parents.

13.2.3 Duration

Section 8 orders subsist until the child reaches 16, unless they are brought to an end earlier by the court, or made of limited duration, s 91(11) CA 1989. They may in exceptional circumstances be extended until the child reaches 18 years of age, s 9(6) CA 1989.

There is no such animal under CA 1989 as an 'interim s 8 order' but instead, only a full order of limited duration, see *S v S (Custody Jurisdiction)* [1995] 1 FLR 155 and also *Re M (Official Solicitor's Role)* [1998] 2 FLR 815.

13.2.4 When the court may not make a s 8 order

(a) Section 9(1) Children Act establishes restrictions on making s 8 orders:

No court shall make any s 8 order, other than a residence order, with respect to a child who is in the care of a local authority.

A residence order will result in the automatic discharge of the care order, s 91(1) CA 1989. A care order automatically discharges a s 8 order, s 91(2) CA 1989.

(b) Section 9(2) states:

No application may be made by a local authority for a residence order or contact order and no court shall make such an order in favour of a local authority

(c)   Section 9(3) imposes restrictions on the application to the court for leave to apply for s 8 orders by some foster parents.

All foster parents need leave of the court to apply for a s 8 order unless they are entitled to apply. If they have fostered the child within the preceding six months they will need the consent of the local authority before seeking leave to apply unless they are related to the child, or the child has lived with them for a period exceeding three years.

(d)   Section 9(4) goes on to provide that 'the period of three years ... need not be continuous, but must have begun not more than five years before the making of the application'.

(e)   Section 9(5)(a) forbids a court to make a specific issue or prohibited steps order 'with a view to achieving a result which could be achieved by making a residence or contact order'.

Specific issue and prohibited steps orders are regarded as quite formidable powers, to be used sparingly and only where appropriate:

(a)   Section 9(5) (b) forbids a court to exercise its power to make a specific issue or prohibited steps order 'in any way which is denied to the High Court (by s 100(2)) in the exercise of its inherent jurisdiction with respect to children'.

(b)   The essential purpose of s 100(2) CA 1989 is to ensure that local authorities seeking some measure of control over a child do so by way of proceedings under Pts IV or V of the Act and not by invoking wardship. Section 9(5)(b) CA 1989 applies the same principle to s 8 proceedings.

(c)   Section 9(6) prohibits the making of any s 8 order which is to have effect for a period which will end after the child has reached the age of 16, unless the circumstances are exceptional. An application in respect of a child with severe learning difficulties or physical mobility problems may well constitute an exception.

13.3 Contact

A contact order means an order requiring the person with whom a child lives, or is to live, to allow the child to visit the person named in the order, or for that person and the child otherwise to have contact with each other.

This order governs contact by direct and indirect means, including visits, staying over, telephone calls, tapes, videos, letters, cards and presents.

Contact orders generally will expire when the child reaches 16, unless there are exceptional circumstances. Contact orders lapse if the parents live continuously together for more than six months, s 11(6) CA 1989. See the new provisions from 1 Dec 2008 under the new s 111 CA 1989 for warnings and enforcement of contact orders, and for 'contact activities' under s. 11 CA 1989.

13.4 Prohibited steps

A prohibited steps order means an order that no step which could be taken by a parent in meeting his parental responsibility for a child, and which is of a kind specified in the order, shall be taken by any person without the consent of the court. This order enables the court to spell out those matters which are to be referred back to it for a decision.

13.5 Residence

A residence order means an order settling the arrangements to be made as to the person with whom the child is to live. Section 11(4) Children Act empowers the court to specify periods of residence in each household involved and for all s. 8 orders under the court may make conditions and directions if necessary to facilitate the implementation of the order. *Re K (shared Residence Order)* [2008] EWCA Civ 526, [2008] 2 FLR 380.

13.5.1 Residence orders and parental responsibility

Residence orders do not remove parental responsibility from anyone else who has it. Parental responsibility can be given to the person in whose favour a residence order is made, remaining while the order is in force, s 12(2) CA 1989, and see above, Chapter 4. Residence orders generally expire when the child reaches 16, unless there are exceptional circumstances, see 13.2.3. above.

Section 12(1) specifically requires the court to make an order under s 4 giving parental responsibility to a father in favour of whom it makes a residence order if he would not otherwise have it. The court may not bring that parental responsibility order to an end while the residence order remains in force, s 12(4). There is an additional effect of the combined operation of s 12(2) and (4) for an unmarried father, which is that discharge of the residence order, or its expiry by effluxion of time will not automatically result in the discharge of his parental responsibility for his child. He continues by implication to have parental responsibility for his child until the child reaches 18, unless it is specifically discharged by court order under s 4(4).

The Act does not allow parental responsibility given under this section to cover agreement to adoption, or a s 18 Adoption Act 1976 application, nor does it permit the appointment of a guardian for the child, s 12(3) CA 1989.

Section 13(1) (b) CA 1989 generally prohibits the removal of a child from the United Kingdom without the written consent of every person who has parental responsibility for the child, or the leave of the court; whilst s 13(2) makes an exception permitting a person in whose favour a residence order is made to take the child abroad for a period of less than one month.

A parent who fears that a child may be removed abroad permanently on the pretext of a short holiday may apply for a prohibited steps order excluding the effect of s 13(2). Where the question of the removal of the child from the jurisdiction is anticipated the court may on the making of a residence order give leave either generally, or for specified purposes, s 13(3).

Where a child is subject to a residence order or to a care order, no person may change that child's surname without the written consent of every person with parental responsibility for that child, or leave of the court, s 13(1)(a) CA 1989. See *Re A (A child: Joint Residence/Parental Responsibility)* [2008] EWCH Civ 867.

13.6 Specific issue

A specific issue order means an order giving directions for the purpose of determining a specific issue which has arisen, or which may arise, in connection with any aspect of parental responsibility for a child.

This order enables either parent to submit a particular dispute to the court for resolution in accordance with the child's best interests. The order was not envisaged as a way of giving one parent the right to determine issues in advance, nor was it intended to be a substitute for a residence or contact order.

13.7 Supplementary provisions

Section 11(1) instructs the court to 'draw up a timetable with a view to determining the question without delay' and 'to give such directions as it considers appropriate for the purpose of ensuring, so far as is reasonably practicable, that the timetable is adhered to'.

Section 11(2) permits rules of court to 'specify periods within which specified steps must be taken in relation to proceedings in which such questions arise' and 'to make other provision ... for the purpose of ensuring, so far as is reasonably practicable, that such questions are determined without delay', see the Family Proceedings Courts (Children Act 1989) Rules 1991 and the Family Court Rules 1991.

Section 11(4) and (5) state:

> Where a court has power to make a s 8 order, it may do so at any time in the course of the proceedings in question, even though it is not in a position to dispose finally of those proceedings.
>
> Where a residence order is made in favour of two or more persons who do not themselves live together, the order may specify the periods during which the child is to live in the different households concerned [s 11(4)].
>
> Where there is a residence order in force, as a result of which the child lives, or is to live, with one of two parents who each have parental responsibility for him, the residence order shall cease to have effect if the parents live together for a continuous period of more than six months [s 11(5)].

Section 11(6) states:

> A contact order which requires the parent with whom a child lives to allow the child to visit, or otherwise have contact with, his other parent shall cease to have effect if the parents live together for a continuous period of more than six months.

Section 8 orders may contain directions, impose conditions, be made for a specified period, or contain provisions for a specified period; and make such incidental, supplemental or consequential provisions as the court thinks fit, s 11(7).

13.8 Practice and procedure in s 8 applications

Procedure is governed in the magistrates' court by the Family Proceedings (Children Act 1989) Rules 1991 SI 1991/1395 (FP(CA) R 1991) and in the county court and High Court by the Family Proceedings Rules 1991 SI 1991/1247 (FPR 1991).

13.8.1 Applications

Freestanding applications should be on form C1, or on form C2 if the application is made in existing 'family proceedings', Sch 1 FP(CA)R 1991 and App 1 FPR 1991.

If the application is for leave only, then, unless it is *ex parte* (see below, 18.6), the applicant for leave needs to complete form C2 giving reasons for the application and requesting leave in writing; and to file and serve the request together with the draft of the application on form C1 to each respondent, see r 3(1) FP(CA)R 1991 and r 4.3(1) FPR 1991.

13.8.2 Venue

Applications may be made at any level. Venue of hearings is governed by the Children (Allocation of Proceedings) Order 1991 SI 1991/1677; and in adoption cases, currently by the Adoption Act 1976.

If children seek leave to apply for a s 8 order, the case should be heard in the High Court, under *Practice Direction (Children Act 1989 – Applications by Children)* [1993] 1 WLR 313; [1993] 1 All ER 820; [1993] 1 FLR 1008.

The Legal Services Commission (formerly the Legal Aid Board) will expect that, wherever possible, the case is commenced in the lowest tier, the Family Proceedings Court, and will seek justification of commencement elsewhere, if there are factors which justify transfer up.

13.8.3 Notice of application for s 8 orders

Under r 4(3) and Sch 2 col (iv) FP(CA)R 1991 and r 4.4(3) App 3 col (iv) FPR 1991, notice shall be served on:

(a)   any local authority providing accommodation for the child;

(b)   anyone with whom the child is living when proceedings commence;

(c)   any person providing refuge in which child is staying;

(d)   any person named in court order, still in effect, relating to child;

(e)   any party to pending proceedings relating to the child;

(f)   every person with whom applicant believes child has lived for three years prior to the application.

Notice of the proceedings is on form C6A, giving the date, time and venue of the hearing. It should be served at least 14 days before the hearing, r 4(3) FP(CA)R 1991 and r 4.4(3) FPR 1991.

13.8.4 Respondents

Under r 7(1) and Sch 2 col (iii) FP(CA)R 1991 and r 4.7(1) and App 3 col (iii) FPR 1991, the following are automatically respondents to a s 8 application:

(a) everyone with parental responsibility for the child;

(b) if a care order is in force, everyone with parental responsibility when the order was made;

(c) parties to proceedings leading to an order for which variation or discharge is now sought.

Respondents should be served with a copy of the application with the date of hearing endorsed on it, together with notice of the proceedings on form C6A. It should be served at least 14 days before the hearing, r 4(1)(b) and Sch 2 col (ii) FP(CA)R 1991 and r 4.4(1)(b), App 3 col (ii) FPR 1991, as amended.

Anyone may apply on form C2 to be joined as respondent, or may be made a respondent by court order without application, see r 7(2) and (5) and FP(CA)R 1991 and rr 4.7(2) and (5) FPR 1991. The same applies if respondents wish to be removed. If the person requesting party status has parental responsibility for the child, the court must grant their request, r 7(4) FP(CA)R 1991 and r 4.7(4) FPR 1991.

13.8.5 Service

Service can be carried out by delivery to the solicitor acting for the person to be served, personally, by document exchange, facsimile transmission, or by first class post; or by delivery to the person himself either personally or by first class post to his last known residence, r 8(1) (a) and (b) FP(CA)R 1991 and r 4.8(1)(a) and (b) FPR 1991.

The court has the power under the rules to abridge, waive or vary the manner of service, r 8(8) FP(CA)R 1991 and r 4.8(8) FPR 1991.

13.8.6 *Ex parte* procedures

These are applications made without requiring the other party/parties to attend on notice. Applications for s 8 orders may be made *ex parte* in any court, r 4(4)(a) FP(CA)R 1991 and r 4.4(4)(a) FPR 1991 but applicants will need leave of the justices clerk in the Family Proceedings Court, r 4(4)(i) FP(CA)R 1991.

Ex parte applications must be supported by the same forms (C1 or C2) which should be brought to court or, if it is a telephone application, they should be filed within 24 hours of the application. In any event, they should be served on the respondents within 48 hours of any order being made. The court has the power under the rules to give directions as to service, see below.

Ex parte residence orders are frowned upon by the courts, and in a number of decisions this has been reiterated: *Re H (A Minor) (Interim Custody)* [1991 2 FLR 411; *Re G (Minors) (ex p Interim Residence Order)* [1993] 1 FLR 910; *Re P (A Minor) (ex p Interim Residence Order)* [1993] 1 FLR 915.

Basically, *ex parte* residence orders should be reserved for extreme urgency, such as child abduction cases. The court referral procedures for urgent applications are set out in a circular from the Lord Chancellor's Department, Guide to Listing Officers, September 1991.

13.8.7 Withdrawal, variation, discharge and appeals

Leave of the court is necessary for withdrawal of s 8 applications (r 5 FP(CA)R 1991 and r 4.5 FPR 1991) on oral application where the children's guardian and the parties are present; or by written request, setting out the reasons for withdrawal, which must then be duly served. The court may permit withdrawal without a hearing if the parties have had a chance to make representations, the views of the children's guardian or court welfare officer have been canvassed, and the court considers it appropriate. The court may direct that a date be set for hearing the application on seven days' notice served on the parties and the children's guardian or court welfare officer.

Applications to vary or discharge a s 8 order may be made by those entitled to seek the original order (see 13.1-43.2 above, and applications at 13.8). The procedure is the same as the original application. Under s 91(14) CA 1989, the court may order that no further application be made without leave.

Section 8 orders are automatically discharged by the making of a care order, or an adoption order, see s 91(2) CA 1989.

An appeal may be lodged with the High Court under s 94(1) Children Act against a decision of a family proceedings court concerning a s 8 order. Appeals against decisions made in the county court and High Court follow the general rules and lie to the Court of Appeal.

13.9 Family assistance order

Section 16 CA 1989 creates the family assistance order, requiring a probation or local authority officer to be made available to `advise, assist and befriend' any person named in the order, s 16(1). But note that the court can only make this order where the circumstances are exceptional, or the court has the consent of every person named in the order save the child, s 16(3).

The person to be 'advised assisted or befriended' may be the child, or his or her parent or guardian, or any person with whom the child is living or who has a contact order-in respect of the child, s 16(2). It originally lasted for six months, but has recently been extended to a possible maximum of 12 months , or a shorter specified period, s 16(5).

The family assistance order may direct the person(s) named in the order to take whatever steps are necessary to enable the officer to be kept informed of their address, and to be allowed to visit the named person, s 16(4).

Where there is in force a family assistance order and also a s 8 order, then the officer may refer to the court the possibility of variation or discharge of the s 8 order, s 16(6). This power should obviously be of use where a family assistance order has been made at the same time as a contact order which is clearly not working.

13.10 Order to local authority to investigate under s 37 CA 1989

Where, in any 'family proceedings', see s 8(3) CA 1989, in which a question arises with respect to the welfare of any child, it appears to the court that it may be appropriate for a care or supervision order to be made, the court may direct the appropriate authority to undertake an investigation of the child's circumstances, s 37(1) CA 1989.

The local authority to whom the direction is given is then under a duty to consider whether it should:

• apply for a care or supervision order;

• provide services or assistance for the child and family;

• take any other action in respect of the child.

If the local authority decides not to seek a care order, it shall inform the court within eight weeks from the s 37 direction of its reasons, any services or assistance provided, and any other action taken. If the decision is made to seek care or supervision, the local authority shall also consider whether it would be appropriate to review the case at a later date, and the date of any such review shall be determined.

Note that all the actions of public authorities, and their failures to act, are subject to compliance with the Human Rights Act 1998 and the European Convention for the Protection of Human Rights and

Fundamental Freedoms, even if the act or omission occurred before the implementation of the Human Rights Act in the UK on 2 October 2000, s 22(4).

The decisions of local authorities may be challenged by complaint or judicial review A decision not to seek a care order may now be subject to challenge under the Human Rights Act and since the courts may not initiate care proceedings, nor make a care order without a local authority application, this may provide another route for redress in situations where it is considered that a care order should have been sought.

14 Commencement and Transfer of Proceedings

14.1 General rules

Under the Family Law Act 1986, a child in respect of whom an application is made must be either ordinarily or habitually resident in England and Wales, or physically present within the jurisdiction of the court at the time of the application. The Family Law Act applies to applications under s 8 CA 1989 1989 (the 'Children Act') and under the inherent jurisdiction of the High Court, but has been extended to care proceedings by case law.

The general rule is that private law applications under CA 1989 may be made at any level of the court, subject to the restrictions of the Legal Aid Board, which would usually prefer the lower cost option.

In public law cases, the general rule is that proceedings should be commenced in the Family Proceedings Court, with specified exceptions, see 14.2 below.

The venue of hearings under the Children Act 1989 and the Adoption and Children Act 2002 is governed by the Children (Allocation of Proceedings) Order 1991 SI 1991/1677; the Children (Allocation of Proceedings) (Appeals) Order 1991 SI 1991/1801; the Family Proceedings (Amendment) Rules 1991 SI 1991/2113; and reference may also be made to the Home Office Circular 45/91 (in *The Children Act 1989 Guidance and Regulations*, Vol 7, p 114).

A checklist of basic commencement provisions is set out at Figure 7 below.

The county courts are divided into categories, each having the power to hear specified types of case. These are Care Centres, Family Hearing Centres and also Divorce Centres. It is also important to ascertain that the court in which the case is to be heard is appropriate. In addition, it is vital to ensure that the judge has power to deal with the case. This is referred to colloquially as having a 'ticket' for the type of proceedings, for example, 'a care ticket'. To check whether a case is appropriate for a category of judge, refer to the *Family Proceedings (Allocation to Judiciary) Directions 1999* as amended in 2003, 2005 and 2007.

14.2 Specified exceptions to the general rules

Under the Children Act (Allocation of Proceedings) Order 1991 SI 1991/1677, public law proceedings may be commenced in the county court or the High Court if:

(a) there are proceedings pending in another court;

(b) there has been a court-directed investigation into the child's circumstances;

(c) the application is for extension, variation or discharge of an existing order.

In these circumstances the application may be made to the court in which the proceedings are pending, or the existing order was made.

14.2.1 Proceedings which must be commenced in the High Court

Case law and practice directions decree that certain proceedings need to be heard at High Court level.

Other cases which should be heard in the High Court include:

(a) applications for authorisation of the use of blood products (for example, where there is religious objection);

(b) issues regarding life saving or life prolonging surgical intervention;

(c) applications for post-adoption contact;

(d) leave to submit a child to HIV tests;

(e) contested issues concerning sterilisation or terminations of pregnancy of minors or mentally ill adults;

(f) cases concerning international issues; and

(g) matters concerning restriction of general publicity.

If a child seeks leave to apply for a s 8 order, the case should be heard in the High Court, under *Practice Direction (Children Act 1989 – Applications by Children)* [1993] 1 WLR 313; [1993] 1 All ER 820; [1993] 1 FLR 1008.

Leave to withhold information from parties is sufficiently serious to warrant High Court hearing, *Re M (Disclosure)* [1998] 2 FLR 1028.

The High Court has the power to refer some cases, with certain exceptions, back to a county court, with consent of the parties or after hearing parties' representations, see *Family Law Act 1996 (Allocation of Proceedings) Order 1997*, art. 12 SI 1997/1896.

14.3 Transfers

Transfers are governed generally by the Children (Allocation of Proceedings) Order 1991 SI 1991/1677.

When proceedings are commenced in one level of the court, they may be transferred up or down the tiers if necessary, subject to the restrictions on venue outlined above. The Children Act Advisory Committee produced a list of 'transfer triggers', see below. These are factors the presence of one or more of which in a case may be persuasive to the court to transfer the matter up. When transferring a case, the court must have regard to the principles in s 1 Children Act, and in particular the avoidance of delay.

14.3.1 The transfer 'trigger' list

The Children Act Advisory Committee has suggested that the presence of one of the factors listed below may give rise to transfer; the presence of two factors is rather more persuasive, and the presence of three or more trigger factors should lead to a transfer:

(a)   Cases which cannot be heard on consecutive days.

(b)   Analysis of conflicting expert evidence.

(c)   Evaluation of psychiatric or medical evidence or allied professional evidence.

(d)   Ritual or multiple sexual abuse.

(e)   Issues affecting recently born babies.

(f)   Multiplicity of children or parties.

(g)   Involvement of more than one local authority.

(h)   Confidential material evidence.

(i)   Cases likely to last longer than two or three days.

(j)   Where delay would occur unless transferred.

(k)   Termination of contact.

(l)   Conflict between children's guardian and child.

(m) Novel issues or facts.

(n)   Conflict between protocols.

(o) Any other circumstance which makes case suitable for higher court.

14.4 Urgent applications

Subject to rules, guidance and case law on jurisdiction and venue (see paras 14.1-14.3 above), the referral procedures for urgent applications are set out in a circular from the Lord Chancellor's Department 'Guide to Listing Officers', September 1991.

Initially, in High Court level cases, under s 9 of the Supreme Court Act the matter can be released to a circuit judge approved to hear Children Act 1989 cases. Some s 9 judges have additional approval to hear care matters. If the matter can be handled by a nominated judge at the local court, this is the preferred route. Where a case is proceeding in, or transferred to the High Court and an urgent hearing is required before a High Court Judge of the Family Division, contact the circuit office. The President of the Family Division's office may arrange for a High Court judge to go out to hear the case. Procedures and names of Family Division Liaison judges are in Children Law and Practice at B[158].

In London, an 'applications judge' sits at the Principal Registry Family Division and at the Royal Courts in normal sitting hours.

As a general rule, circuits should deal with matters arising on Friday evenings, weekends, public and privilege holidays.

The Royal Courts of Justice will take urgent cases at County Court and High Court level with 24 hours cover every day of the year, including weekday evenings and nights, and also may in special need, provide a circuit judge at weekends and public and privilege holidays.

The out of hours contact number of the Royal Courts of Justice is 0207 947 6000. The security officer will, on request, refer the caller to the urgent business officer for the day.

The urgent business officer needs to know:

(a)   the type of application;

(b)   circumstances of the case.

He will decide whether the case merits contacting one of the three members of the judiciary on duty, at the appropriate level, and he will then return the call within 10–15 minutes. The judge dealing with the matter will advise on how the application should be handled.

For urgent County Court applications, contact the local County Court Family Hearing Centre.

Figure 7: Commencement of proceedings

Children Act 1989 Section	Order	Applicant	Needs leave	Form	Court can make order of own volition	Family Proceedings Court	County Court	High Court
4	Parental responsibility	Child's father		C1 or C2		Children (Allocation of Proceedings) Order 1991 SI 1991/1677, Home Office Circular 45/91		
4(3)	Termination of PR	Person with PR Child	✓	C1 or C2			Applicant's choice, subject to legal aid restrictions	
5	Appoint Guardian	Anyone		C1 or C2	✓		Applicant's choice, subject to legal aid restrictions	
6	Terminate appt of Guardian	Anyone with PR Child	✓	C1 or C2			Applicant's choice, subject to legal aid restrictions	
8	Contact	Parent Guardian Person with Residence Order Party to marriage Person with care of child for 3 years or consent of those with PR	Anyone with leave may apply	C1 or C2	✓	Applicant's choice, subject to legal aid restrictions		Child's application for leave
8	Residence	Parent Guardian Person with Residence Order Party to marriage Person with care of child for 3 years or consent of those with PR	Anyone with leave may apply	C1 or C2	✓	Applicant's choice, subject to legal aid restrictions		Child's application for leave
8	Prohibited Steps	Parent Guardian Person with Residence Order	*Anyone with leave may apply	C1 or C2	✓	Applicant's choice, subject to legal aid restrictions		Child's application for leave HIV tests Restriction of publicity International dimension

Children Act 1989 Section	Order	Applicant	Needs leave	Form	Court can make order of own volition	Family Proceedings Court	County Court	High Court
8	Specific Issue	Parent / Guardian / Person with Residence Order	* Anyone with leave may apply	C1 or C2	✓	Applicant's choice, subject to legal aid restrictions		Child seeks leave & able child disabled blood products use / HIV tests / Restriction of publicity / International dimension
16	Family Assistance Order	Can only be made on the courts' volition with consent of the parties			✓	← Any court →		
25	Secure Accommodation	Local Authority / Area Health Auth. / NHS Trust / Person caring in a residential home		C1 + Supplement C20		√E	E = EXCEPTIONS: * Court directed investigations * Pending proceedings	
31	Care Order or Supervision Order	Local Authority or NSPCC		C1, C2 + Suppl C13		√E	* Extension variation or discharge of existing order	
34	Care Contact Order	Local Authority / Child / Anyone with leave		C1 or C2	Court can make s 34 order along with Care Order	√E	May be commenced in the court in which direction given, proceedings are pending, or original order was made	
36	Education Supervision Order	Local Education Authority		Form C17 or C17A		√E		
43	Child Assessment Order	Local Authority or NSPCC		C1 + Suppl C16		√E		
44	Emergency Protection	Any Person		C1 with Suppl C11		√E		
50	Recovery Order	Person with PR by care order or Emergency Protection order / Designated Officer		C1 with Suppl C18		√E		

15 Working With Children

15.1 Appointment and role of the children's guardian

The children's guardian is a person appointed by the court to act for a child aged under 18 years, or an adult who needs such assistance. In cases under the Children Act 1989 (CA 1989), a children's guardian should be appointed in 'specified family proceedings' (see s 41(6) CA 1989 and 15.1.1 below) unless satisfied that it is not necessary to do so; and may be appointed in certain non-specified proceedings.

The children's guardian should be independent and has a duty to investigate the circumstances of the case thoroughly, interviewing parties and witnesses and examining all available evidence. The children's guardian should interview all those who may be able to give relevant information about the child's life and circumstances and also the child and her family, and may request any necessary further information or assessments and then evaluate all the evidence. The children's guardian has a duty to advise the court of the child's wishes and feelings; to inform the court of the child's circumstances, bearing in mind the welfare check list; to evaluate all the options open to the court; and finally to advise the court on the best way forward in the interests of the child.

Children's guardians may be employees of CAFCASS, or they may be independent social workers who have a contractual arrangement with CAFCASS for the taking of cases, (but not employed by) CAFCASS. See Chapter 4 at section 4.7. for information about the Children and Family Court Advisory and Support Service (CAFCASS), which comprises the former Children's Guardian and Reporting Officer Service; the Family Court Welfare Service; and the Children's Branch of the Official Solicitor's Department.

Information can be obtained from the CAFCASS government website at www.cafcass.gov.uk and at the website for NAGALRO (the organisation for guardians and reporting officers), www.nagalro.com.

The Official Solicitor may be appointed as children's guardian, and the role of the Official Solicitor is set out in Practice Note [1999] 1 FLR 310.

The provisions governing the appointment and functioning of a children's guardian are in ss 41-42 CA 1989 and rr 10 and 11 Family Proceedings Court (Children Act) Rules 1991 SI 1991/1395 and rr 4.10 and 4.11 Family Proceedings Rules 1991 SI 1991/1247.

A child who is subject to 'specified proceedings' is entitled to free legal representation under the legal aid scheme. A solicitor may be appointed for the child by the children's guardian or by the court. A child of sufficient understanding may wish to choose their own solicitor, which is acceptable provided that the appointment complies with CA 1989 and rules cited above.

The children's guardian has access under s 42(1) CA 1989 to all social work files and records and, if any of these documents are copied by the children's guardian, they are admissible in evidence before the court, s 42 (2).

See the case of *Re T* [1994] 1 FLR 632 in which the local authority refused to disclose records of potential adopters to the children's guardian, but the Court of Appeal ordered that the children's guardian should have access to them under the terms of s 42 CA 1989.

Note the leading case of *Oxfordshire CC v P* [1995] 1 FLR 582 concerning the issue of how confidential information should be treated by children's guardians.

The children's guardian may ask for access to medical or psychiatric records of the child, and may wish to see the health records of others involved in the child's life.

The report of the children's guardian is confidential to the court and the parties and leave is required to disclose it to others, or to withhold information from parties. Leave to withhold information from parties is sufficiently serious to warrant High Court hearing, *Re M (Disclosure)* [1998] 2 FLR 1028.

The children's guardian in specified proceedings may bring applications on behalf of the child, or the child's solicitor, if the child is of sufficient age to instruct separately (see 15.2 below).

See also *The Children Act 1989 Guidance and Regulations* Vol 7 (1989); *The Children Act Advisory Committee Handbook of Best Practice in Children Act Cases* (1997); and *The Representation of Children in Public Law Proceedings, Law Society's Guidance* (October 2006) approved by the ALC and *Resolution*, formerly the SFLA.

15.1.1 Specified proceedings

Specified proceedings are defined in s 41(6) CA 1989.

Specified proceedings include applications for parental orders under s 30 of the Human Fertilisation and Embryology Act 1990.

15.2 Conflict between children's guardian and child

The child, if of sufficient age and understanding, may request client confidentiality with their solicitor, and/or disagree with the recommendations of the children's guardian.

In this case, the child's solicitor must decide (a) whether the child is of sufficient age and understanding to instruct separately, and (b) whether there is a conflict between the child and the children's guardian. If both factors are present, the solicitor should discuss the matter with the children's guardian. Under rr 11 and 12(1)(a) Family Proceedings Court (Children Act 1989) Rules 1991 SI 1991/1395 and rr 4.11 and 4.12(1)(a) Family Proceedings Rules 1991 SI 1991/1247, if a child radically disagrees with the children's guardian, and is able to instruct his or her own solicitor, then the court must be informed, and the solicitor continues to represent the child client. The children's guardian will then proceed unrepresented, or seek another lawyer where necessary.

The child of sufficient age may ask their solicitor to keep matters confidential, and disclosure is then an issue for the solicitor to decide. The Law Society (*The Representation of Children in Public Law Proceedings* (October 2006)) allows a solicitor to breach the confidentiality of an immature child client where there is a risk of serious harm to the child or to others, but the guidance suggests that a mature ('*Gillick* competent') child may be entitled to confidentiality unless other children are at risk, or the child is in fear of their life or serious injury.

Another possible way to avoid ethical dilemmas for solicitors representing children (or adults in family matters) is to gain the client's agreement at the outset of taking instructions, that, if a concern arises of a risk of serious harm to the client or to others, the solicitor has permission to disclose the concerns to the children's guardian, or to an appropriate helping agency. This sort of agreement is often used by other professionals. Clients are usually willing to give their consent, and this avoids any ethical difficulty. Clients, especially young people and children, usually tell people they trust about their problems because they would like to have help. If they want to keep it secret, discuss their reasons for this. Are they afraid of reprisals, or possibly protecting someone else? Is there anyone else they feel they could trust with this information? Once we know what their fear is, we can talk over resources and referrals which are acceptable to the client. Their worry is often that the helping agencies, once told about it, might let them down by failing to provide the help needed. We can do something about that by agreeing to stay alongside the client and doing our best to ensure that they do receive effective and appropriate help, in the ways they feel are right for them.

15.3 Should I see my child client?

Lawyers representing children should, as a matter of good practice, meet with their child clients, unless, exceptionally, there is good reason not to do so. Necessary arrangements should be made in co-operation with the children's guardian, the child's parents and carers, and the local authority.

We agree with *Acting for Children* by Christine Liddle (1992), pp 5-6:

> Although children vary in their ability to give instructions, it is still very beneficial to the solicitor's understanding of the case for him to meet his child client, whatever the age.

Legal aid in public law proceedings is granted to the child client, through the children's guardian. Initially, the solicitor is instructed through the children's guardian, but will need, as a vital part of the preparation of the case, to speak with child clients who appear to be of sufficient maturity to discover, firstly, whether the child is sufficiently mature to instruct separately if necessary, and, secondly, whether a conflict exists between the child and the children's guardian. The solicitor also needs to elicit the child's wishes and feelings in order to represent them to the court.

Solicitors and children's guardians both need to meet child clients:

> If a solicitor is to represent a child properly in court, it is necessary to understand the child's personality, behaviour, background and needs. This can be done through information gained by others, but it is best done at first hand. Even a small baby can non-verbally tell the observer a good deal about herself. Seeing a child in his environment and interacting with him gives not only greater understanding of the child but also a sense of involvement with the client which makes the task so much more personal, and gives encouragement to the solicitor act for the child as a person, rather than as an 'object of concern' or 'a case'. Liddle (1992)

In October 1994, the Solicitors Family Law Committee produced *Guidance for Solicitors Acting for Children under the Children Act 1989.* This guidance comments that a solicitor's professional training is not well designed to equip him or her to make an assessment of a child's understanding unaided, although solicitors, particularly those on the Children Panel, will have a certain amount of knowledge through experience and/or will have undergone some training in child development.

Clearly, the expectation is that solicitors will at least discuss the issue of competence with the experts in the case, and this principle should apply equally in public law cases. The children's guardian in a public law case is the first person to be consulted on the issue. Child psychologists, psychiatrists, counsellors and others working with the child will also have useful views.

'*Gillick* competence' evolved from the case of *Gillick v West Norfolk and Wisbech HA and DSS* [1986] AC 112 and is vitally important (see above, 12.1.2).

See also the *Guide to Good Practice for Solicitors Acting for Children* (2000) E para 1:

> When acting for a child, the solicitor should always meet the child and due regard should be taken for the most appropriate setting and style for such a meeting. Interviews should be short and at the child's pace.

Pat Monro and Lis Forrester assume that solicitors will meet their child clients, adding practical advice:

> Where a young child is involved, the instructions will come from the children's guardian and it will usually be appropriate for the children's guardian to meet with the child in the first instance without the solicitor, who can be introduced at a later date. A young child will probably be confused by the introduction of a number of new faces, and therefore it is important for the children's guardian to get to know the child before the solicitor becomes involved.

See Monro, P and Forrester, L, *The Children's Guardian* (1995) p 46.

Note: There are very rare cases where it may be inappropriate for the solicitor to see the child, for example where the child is severely emotionally damaged and the introduction of a new face may adversely affect his therapeutic progress.

15.4 Taking instructions and communicating with children

Good communication with children is essential if instructions are to be effective. A basic understanding of child development, confidence in being with children (preferably accrued with practical experience) and integrity are vital. Children dislike being patronised, and they will see through prevarication. They deserve the respect of straight answers to any questions they ask, given in age appropriate language.

Older child clients may like to receive an age appropriate letter to let them know that they have a solicitor and to provide a channel of communication which they can take up themselves if they are worried or curious or simply want to communicate about anything. Solicitors may communicate by telephone, mobile or emails with older children. A few stamped envelopes (addressed to the solicitor's office) plus a mobile telephone number and an email address sent with the introductory letter enable the child to telephone, text or write back if she wishes. It also empowers her – she has the information and the means to communicate and respond – so she will not be reliant on others to get in touch with her solicitor, and she can get in touch confidentially and quickly if necessary.

Many younger children like to send their solicitor a drawing, and to receive a reply is a great boost for their confidence. Space may be needed on the office walls for the many drawings that will inevitably accumulate!

Everyone has their own way of communicating with others, so there are no hard and fast rules. A few guidelines which may be of use are set out below.

15.4.1 Communication with children

* Discuss the timing of the first meeting with the child with the children's guardian and whether to go with them on the first visit to the child.

* Find out what the children's guardian has already told the child about the case and about the role of children's guardian and solicitor and how much of the facts it is appropriate to tell the child or to discuss with her.

* Explain clearly and honestly issues of confidentiality to the child in age-appropriate language.

* Children do not like being patronised.

- Informal clothing is best, not formal or intimidating 'power dressing' clothes, but you should look professional. Get on a level with young clients, maybe even sit on the floor to talk/play!

- Take a few props to help communication: a selection from these may be useful: paper, crayons or pencils (never felt tips or your best fountain pen), pipe cleaners, a glove puppet, a few small toys, a family of dolls, toy bus/car, toy telephone, etc.

But do not worry, if you don't feel at ease playing with toys ... it's also totally ok to just *talk* with children!

- Do not take sweets, food or felt tipped pens (these can upset carers, tummies, or ruin furniture!).

- What does the child wish to be called? Names are important. Does the child have preferred names for himself or others?

- Try to understand the child, get them to talk about favourite/least favourite television programmes, activities, pop stars, food, colours, clothes, football teams, toys, friends, people and pets.

- Usually, the guardian will have introduced the solicitor to the child, but if not, then, once the child is at ease, explain your role as their solicitor. Many older children have seen lawyers on television and have varying ideas about the legal system, ranging from the Dickensian to the American, or scenes from *The Bill* or *Judge John Deed*. The explanation needs to be age appropriate. It could be something along these lines:

  > I am your solicitor. Part of my job is to go along to the court and talk to the judge (or magistrates) and to tell them how you feel about what is happening now, and what you would like to happen. I would like to talk with you and want to listen to what you want to say ...

There will be much more to explain and discuss with a child client, but this is a start!

- Explain to the child what the proceedings are about, in an age appropriate way.

- Do not overtire a young child, or overstay: an hour or less is usually enough.

- Do not try to press a child for facts, especially about past traumatic events, as it may cause emotional distress, which their carers then have to deal with afterwards. Avoid questioning a child intrusively. Involve the child's carers if help is needed to engage the child; and end the visit if the child seems unwilling to continue. Never distress a child by being 'pushy' if they do not want to talk, or by overstaying. The children's guardian will assist with advice, help or, if the solicitor is unsure, a joint visit to the child can be made.

* A sense of calm, goodwill and appropriate humour helps!

15.5 Child development

There is not space in this book to discuss child development in any detail. There are a number of excellent reference books on the market, some of which are listed in Chapter 19 below.

The contribution by Mary Sheridan in Appendix 1 to *Assessing Children in Need and their Families* (2000) contains concise, useful information on child development from birth to five years.

Another useful book for lawyers used by children's guardians is *Child Development – Diagnosis and Assessment* by Holt, KS (1994).

The *ABC of One to Seven* and the *ABC of Child Protection*, published by the British Medical Association, are useful and many bookshops carry a range of books on child development intended for parents which practitioners will find readable and helpful.

15.6 Understanding your child client – race, religion, culture and ethnicity

The welfare checklist pays attention to the child's 'physical educational and emotional needs', s 1 (3)(b) CA 1989; and 'age, sex, background and any characteristics of his which the court considers relevant', s 1(3) (d) CA 1989.

Although CA 1989 did not refer specifically to race, religion and culture, they are clearly included in these categories. If the child's background, and needs arising from it, is not clear to the solicitor and children's guardian, then expert assistance should be sought from someone who fully understands the child's cultural, religious and social needs. The child may also have physical needs which may have to be explained to a carer from a different culture, for example, food, religious taboos and customs, hair and skin care, etc. Quite often, behaviour which would not make sense within one culture in a given situation makes perfect sense when understood in the context of another. The court must take the child's needs fully into account when deciding the most appropriate way forward to promote and safeguard the child's welfare.

15.7 After the case is over

Children often develop a relationship of trust with their solicitor, and, whatever the outcome of the case, will frequently keep in touch. The children's guardian's role for the child ceases when the final order is made. By contrast, the solicitor is a continuing source of help and a useful contact in the outside world. Children may be pleased to have their own solicitor whom they can contact or ask about problems as they arise, particularly as they reach their teenage years.

It is good to have a final visit to a child client and to let them have a business card to keep if they are old enough to use it. A few sheets of blank paper, and stamped addressed envelopes can be left in case the child wants to write. They may want to phone, text or call into the office. If a child makes contact, make a point of responding immediately, and in a way appropriate for the child's age and understanding.

Children who are in care need to know their rights, and these should have been explained by the social services department. If a child is concerned about the standard of care, or has a need to complain, the solicitor may be the first person they think of to tell about their problem. Older children may at some time wish to instruct a solicitor on their own behalf to apply for a s 8 order, or to apply to discharge a care order, so it is essential to keep an avenue of communication open for them.

Often the child may be concerned about an aspect of their care, and the solicitor can perform a useful function in explaining and mediating between the child and parents or agencies when difficulties arise.

Older children on leaving care also have the right to additional services on leaving care under the *Children (Leaving Care) Act* 2000, and they may wish to seek advice about the ways in which their needs can be met.

Case records, statements and documents should be kept at least until the child reaches 21. In adoption cases, records may need to be kept longer. Guardians working from home are required to return their case papers to CAFCASS for archiving and are not permitted to retain any information at all in relation to the case, including copies of reports that they have written. Thus if there are future applications it may be rather crucial that the child's solicitor has retained a full set of papers, particularly if the previous guardian is not available or if the archiving system is unable to quickly locate old papers.

It goes without saying that cases are confidential and need to be kept (and eventually destroyed) securely.

15.8 Judges seeing children in private law proceedings

Judges should be very carful about when and how they see children in the course of private law proceedings.

In the recent case of *Re W* [2008] EWCA Civ 538; [2008] All ER (D) 258 (May), the Court of Appeal gave useful guidance on this in relation to a judge seeing a child of 15 years of age:

* Decision to see a child or not is in the discretion of the court.

* Use that discretion cautiously.

* Recommended time and place is in chambers after submissions.

* The child should be seen at court.

* The judge should not promise confidentiality.

* The judge should summarise the salient points of the interview for parties, so that they can deal with it.

A reading of the full judgment in this case is recommended, along with the Law Society's 2006 *Guidance*, mentioned in this chapter.

16 Assessment of Children in Need and Care Planning

16.1 New developments and materials

In 2000, the government has brought in the Quality Protects Programme, to 'ensure that referral and assessment processes discriminate effectively between different types and level of need, and produce a timely response' (John Hutton, Minister of State for Social Services, March 2000). To facilitate the implementation of the Quality Protects Programme, the Department of Health set up steering and advisory groups and the Departments of Health, Education, Employment and the Home Office issued new materials to provide guidance, practice material, and training resources. The emphasis is on evidence-based practice, and careful consideration of the needs of the individual child, with an expectation that inter-agency child protection and social work practice is based on analysis, reflection, and sound judgment in decision making.

Two major assessment materials are the companion volumes, *Framework for the Assessment of Children in Need and their Families* (2000) and *Assessing Children in Need and Their Families – Practice Guidance* (2000). Both of these are essential reference material for child protection practice. They replace the old 'Orange Book', *Protecting Children: A Guide to Social Workers Undertaking a Comprehensive Assessment* (1988), but they still refer to Mary Sheridan's very useful basic child development charts for children from birth to five years.

Additional resources are the range of *Initial and Core Assessment Records* (2000) for children of different age groups and the *Family Assessment Pack of Questionnaires and Scales* (2000).

Note that the new *Working Together to Safeguard Children* (2006) replaces all earlier versions.

The *Family Assessment Pack of Questionnaires and Scales* is a contribution to the assessment process by Cox and Bentovim, providing a set of measurement scales for different family situations including questionnaires on:

- strengths and difficulties (screening for emotional and behavioural problems);

- parenting daily hassles (screening for parenting stressors);

- adult well being (screening for irritability, depression and anxiety);

- home conditions (family cleanliness, etc);

- adolescent well-being (for self rating for depression);

- family activity (in different age bands, 2-6 and 7-12 years) (child-centredness);

- recent life events (life events as potential stressors);

- alcohol scale (screening for alcohol overuse);

- two more measuring instruments will be available later, the *Home Inventory* and the *Assessment of Family Competence, Strengths and Difficulties*. These will be available for practitioners and in training programmes.

16.1.2   Training materials

- *The Child's World, Assessing Children in Need, Training and Development Pack* (2000), put together by the NSPCC and the University of Sheffield, is also available from the DoH. It contains a video, training guide, and a reader.

- *Crossing Bridges – Training Resources for Working with Mentally Ill Parents and their Children.*

- *Making an Impact – Children and Domestic Violence.*

- *Turning Points – Resource Pack for Communicating with Children.*

- *In on the Act – Training Programme for Relevant Professionals.*

- Family Group Conferences.

- *Unaccompanied Asylum-Seeking Children: A Training Pack.*

- *Looking After Children – Training Resource Pack.*

- *Management and Implementation Guide.*

- Training Guide.

- Training Video.

- Video Notes.

- Reader.

•   Demonstration Documents.

CAFCASS has introduced a plethora of 'tools' for working with both children and adults. These include the *Needs Wishes and Feelings Pack*, and the *Domestic Violence Tool Kit*.

16. 2 The Assessment Framework

A child who is at risk of harm is by definition deemed to be 'a child in need'. Therefore all the guidance materials listed above apply to children who are subject to care proceedings, and also apply to many other children who may be assessed for the provision of resources by a local authority under s 17 and Sch 2 to the Children Act 1989.

In *Assessing Children in Need and Their Families*, the assessment framework is depicted for clarity in the form of a triangle. The child and the safeguarding and promoting of his welfare is central to the assessment process. Each limb of the triangle thus represents a particular area or domain of the child's world, which is further broken down into that domain's component parts, all of which inter- relate, and all of which need careful consideration both at an individual level and then as the whole picture.

Figure 8: the child assessment framework

The key areas are:

(a) the child's developmental needs, which broadly looks at his emotional, social and behavioural development and function including a consideration of his identity. This area also considers the child's physical health, his self care skills and his educational development;

(b) the second limb considers the parenting capacity of the child's carers and as might be expected includes an appraisal of the provision of basic care, nurture, stimulation, guidance and boundaries, stability and emotional warmth;

(c) the third domain considers family and environmental factors, including the family history and functioning, the wider family, housing, employment, income, the family's social integration and the availability of community resources.

The structure of this assessment framework has been specifically designed to provide a systematic method for the gathering and analysing of information about children, in order that different types and levels of need can be more effectively identified.

Assessing Children in Need and Their Families looks also at the needs of children from other cultural and ethnic groups. The Practice Guidance points out that this assessment model is equally applicable to disabled children and their families, however the needs of the carers should be a particular factor to be taken into account.

The chapters each contain a significant body of reference material for further reading and research. The final chapter looks at resources to assist effective assessment, introducing the *Family Assessment Pack of Questionnaires and Scales*, and setting out the principles for use of the materials. The age-related set of *Assessment Records* produced by the DoH are an additional assessment tool.

See also *The Children Act Now: Messages from Research* (1999) which summarises the major Department of Health commissioned studies on CA 1989.

16.3 Care planning

Practitioners should note that case law precedent has already established the requirement for a care plan in s 31 applications. The emphasis now is on the nature, format and content of the care plan. See also Chapter 7.

More time is spent in the consideration of the care plan than almost any other aspect of care proceedings. It is far less likely that there will be a contest over the threshold criteria, than a dispute over the proposed plan for the child.

Practitioners need to have a copy of Local Authority Circular LAC (99) 29, entitled *Care Plans and Care Proceedings under the Children Act 1989*. Issued on the 12 August 1999, it sets out the format and content of the care plans upon which the courts expect to base their consideration of the appropriate order to make in care proceedings. The circular is issued under s 7 of the Local Authority Social Services Act 1970, which requires local authorities to act under the guidance of the Secretary of State, and it supplements Vol 3 *Residential Care*, and Vol 4 *Family Placements* of *The Children Act 1989 Guidance and Regulations*.

The circular sets out the contents of the care plan, in five sections:

(a)   overall aim;

(b)   child's needs including contact;

(c)   views of others;

(d)   placement details and timetable;

(e)   management and support by local authority.

Each child must have their own individual care plan, this also applies to sibling groups. The plan must be a separate document, and in the case of a final care plan should not only be signed by the social worker responsible for compiling the plan, but should also be endorsed by one or more 'relevant senior officers' from within the local authority.

The local authority should provide interim care plans in order that the court has the necessary information available before making interim orders. The circular indicates that during proceedings the numbering of care plans is desirable to reduce confusion, and to ensure that parties know which care plan is in operation.

The format of the care plan is set out in detail at paras 15-18. There is comment about care plans and assessment which relates to the new framework for the assessment of children in need (para 23), comment about the needs of disabled children (para 26), race, culture, religion and language (para 27) and care planning prior to adoption (paras 28-33).

Copies of LAC (99)29 can be obtained from the DoH, PO Box 777, London SE1 6XH, or from the website at www.open.gov.uk/ doh/ dhome.htm. Other recent circulars can also be obtained from this website.

16.4 Adoption issues

The Adoption law has been reformed, and a raft of new legislation has been developed. It is not within the ambit of this book to discuss adoption in detail, but for reference, please see the following:

*   Adoption and Children Act 2002
*   Adoption and Children (Scotland) Act 2007
*   Adoption Support Agencies (England) and Adoption Agencies (Miscellaneous Amendments) Regulations 2005, S.I. 2005/2720
*   Adoption Agencies Regulations 2005, S.I. 2005/389
*   Adoption Agencies (Wales) Regulations 2005, S.I. 2005/1313
*   Adoption (Bringing Children into the United Kingdom) Regulations 2003 S.I. 2003 /1173
*   Adoption Information and Intermediary Services Regulations (pre-commencement) 2005, S.I. 2005/890
*   Adoption Support Services Regulations 2005, S.I. 2005/691
*   Adoptions with a Foreign Element Regulations 2005 S.I. 2002 /392

There are a number of excellent publications which explain the new law and practice, listed at the end of this book.

17 Appeals and Enforcement

17.1 Appeals and judicial review

Appeals are discussed briefly in these practice notes under each topic, but since there is limited space, judicial review, complaints procedures and appeals procedures can only be mentioned, giving further references. Hershman and McFarlane have an excellent section on judicial review and appeals in Vol 1, s I. Other useful books are: Manning, J, *Judicial Review Proceedings* (2004); Fordham, M, *Judicial Review Handbook* (2008); and Paynter, ER, *Applicant's Guide to Judicial Review* (2008).

17.1.1 Family proceedings court appeals to the County Court

There is no 'slip rule', and no power to review or re-hear a decision. What is pronounced by the chair of the Bench must be written up as the order, and amendment can only happen if the words are not accurately written down. Since 6 April 2009, Family Proceedings Court orders under the Children Act 1989 and the Adoption and Children Act 2002 are now challenged by notice of appeal to the county court within 21 days, see s 111-112 of the Access to Justice (Destination of Appeals) (Family Proceedings) Order 2009, SI 2009/871.

17.1.2 County court appeals

Appeal lies from decisions of the district judge to a judge of the same court, r 4.22(4) Family Proceedings Rules 1991.

The county court has the power to review interim, *ex parte* or interlocutory orders; or to rehear its own decisions where there has been no error of the court. In other cases there may be an application to discharge the order, or the parties may serve notice of appeal within 14 days of the decision to the Court of Appeal and are governed by RSC Ord 59.

Figure 9: Table of enforcement procedures for Children Act orders

Breach of Order	Injunction/Penal Notice	Surety/Bond	Committal or Contempt	Other remedy available	Police Powers and Criminal Proceedings
Refusal to give up a child for Residence Order			RSC Ord 45 r 7 CCR Ord 29 r 1 High Court or County Court may commit Family Proc Court may use s 63(3) MCA 1980	Search and Recovery Order s 34 Family Law Reform Act 1986 'Seek & Find' High Court Inherent jurisdiction	
Threat to remove child from UK, or actual removal attempt		can be used to ensure return of child	as above	1) Port Alert System 2) Passport Restriction	1) Police duty to assist where threat of danger or breach of the peace 2) Child Abduction & Custody Act 1985 offence
Change of name when child subject to residence order w/o consent or leave	✓		✓		
Refusal to comply with s 8 Contact Order	To use penal notice the acts to be enforced must be set out clearly in the order		Committal is rare, but possible	S 11(7) Directions, including contact activities; also s 111 CA 1989 warnings and enforcement	
Breach of specific issue or prohibited steps	✓		✓		Police duty to assist where threat of danger may be used in medical emergency
Removal of child from care (under s 31 order)	If removal from jurisdiction is threatened		✓	Port alert if threat to remove from UK High Court Tipstaff if threat to remove from jurisdiction Recovery order s 50 Children Act 1989	Child Abduction & Custody Act 1985 offence Police duty to assist where threat of danger may be used in medical emergency
Change of name of child in s 31 care without leave/consent	✓		✓		
Failure to produce records to guardian ad litem in care/supervision proceedings	Application to produce documents under s 42 Children Act 1989		Application to court to produce documents under s 42 Children Act 1989		
Breach of directions of the court in Children Act 1989 proceedings, as to filing, service or attendance				• Wasted Costs Order • Court may impose adjournment, or proceed in absence of party • Evidence may be disallowed – but rare in Children Act cases	

17.1.3 High Court appeals

Appeal lies from decisions of a district judge to a judge of the same court, for rehearing, no leave required, RSC Ord 58 r 1.

The High Court has the power to review interim, *ex parte* or interlocutory orders; or to rehear its own decisions where there has been no error of the court, s 17 of the Supreme Court Act. In other cases there may be an application to discharge the order, or the parties may serve notice of appeal within 14 days of the decision to the Court of Appeal. Procedure is governed by Ord 59 Rules of the Supreme Court.

Occasionally, appeals may 'leapfrog' by certificate granted under s 12(1) of the Administration of Justice Act 1969 direct to the House of Lords.

17.2 Complaints procedures

If any person wishes to complain about any action by the Department of Social Services in relation to a child, the procedure is set out in the Representations Procedure (Children) Regulations 1991 SI 1991/894. The policies which underpin the rights of 'service users', and the way in which complaints should be handled, are set out in: Vols 1-9 of The *Children Act 1989 Guidance and Regulations; The Care of Children, Principles and Practice in Regulations and Guidance* (1991); and Department of Health and Social Services Inspectorate, *The Right to Complain* (1991).

17.2.1 Family proceedings court appeals lie to the County Court (from 6 April 2009)

There is no 'slip rule', and no power to review or rehear a decision.

What is pronounced by the chair of the Bench must be written up as the order, and amendment can only happen if the words are not accurately written down. Orders are challenged by notice of appeal within 21 days to the County Court under the *Access to Justice (Destination of Appeals) (Family Proceedings) Order* 2009, amending s 94(1) *Children Act, Ord* 55 r 1(1)(2) *Rules of the Supreme Court* and r 4.22 *Family Proceedings Rules* 1991, SI 1991/1247. Check with the County Court the time currently allowed for appeal against interim care of supervision orders.

17.3 Enforcement

Enforcement of orders made under CA 1989 is discussed briefly in these practice notes under each topic. Further detail is available from

Hershman and McFarlane's *Children Law and Practice*, which has an excellent section on enforcement of Children Act orders in Vol 1, and a helpful table of enforcement procedures for Children Act orders.

18 Expert Evidence

18.1 Instructing expert witnesses

An 'expert witness' has no legal definition. Many professionals style themselves as 'expert witnesses', but it is the court which makes the final decision as to who is accepted as an expert in a particular specialist field. Experts are privileged in the eyes of the law – they are not restricted to evidence of fact and can give their opinion on any relevant matter in which they are appropriately qualified. Acceptance of a specialist as an expert, therefore, will vary according to the issues in each case, and to assess expertise, it is expected that the expert will outline their experience and qualifications for the court.

Refusal of permission to call an expert may prejudice the right of the party to a fair trial under Article 6 of the ECHR – see the case of *Elsholz v Germany* (2002) 34 EHRR 58; [2000] 2FLR 486.

The choice of the appropriate expert for a case is never an easy one – and even then, choice may be limited by availability and time frames. See below at 18.4 for ideas derived from practice.

In the course of proceedings in the High Court, Wall J has given helpful guidance on the use of expert witnesses in his judgments – *Re M (Minors) (Care Proceedings: Children's Wishes)* [1994] 1 FLR 749 and *Re G (Minors) (Expert Witnesses)* [1994] 2 FLR 291, and with Iain Hamilton, in *A Handbook for Expert Witnesses in Children Act Cases* (2000). Written for witnesses, but also good reading for lawyers, they set out in detail the way in which experts can expect to be approached, issues concerning disclosure, the preparation of instructions and reports.

See also the *Handbook of Best Practice in Children Act Cases*, Children Act Advisory Committee (1997) and *Children Law and Practice* at Section N.

The Public Law Outline: The Court Companion (Pressdee et al, 2008) provides an excellent comprehensive guide to the PLO.

The *Practice Direction: Experts in Family Proceedings Relating to Children. 13 February, 2008* (EFPRC 2008 para 2.1.) (referred to below as *Practice Direction: Experts 2008*) as came into force on 1 April 2008, and applies to all:

•   Placement and adoption proceedings;

And the following family proceedings held in private:

- High Court's exercise of its jurisdiction in relation to children;

- Proceedings under CA 1989 in any family court;

- High Court and county court proceedings in relation to maintenance or upbringing of a minor.

The practice direction can be found in full at section N of *Children Law and Practice*, and on the web at www.hmcourts-service.gov.uk/cms/files/Experts-PD-flagB-final-version-14-01-08.pdf.

The Civil Evidence Act 1972 applies to family proceedings in the High Court, county court and the family court (s 5). The rules relating to expert evidence in Children Act 1989 (the 'Children Act') cases are the Family Proceedings Courts (Children Act) Rules 1989, r 18 and the Family Proceedings Rules 1989, r 4.18; the Rules of the Supreme Court, Ord 38, rr 35-44; and the County Court Rules, Ord 20, rr 27-28. Pt 35 of the Civil Procedure Rules 1998 also now applies to ancillary relief applications in Children Act cases.

18.1.2   Expert instruction checklist

Leave, consents and preliminary enquiries of experts

- When considering which expert to instruct, the court needs some information about the experts to decide which is appropriate.

- The experts may need some information about the case to decide whether to accept instructions. Provision of such anonymised information will not require prior consent, see *Practice Direction: Experts 2008* at 1.7. BUT if experts need to check on the names of the parties for conflicts of interest before accepting instructions, consent to disclose the names would be required.

- Obtain all necessary leave for instruction of expert and for examination of a child before instructing the expert (see Family Proceedings Courts (Children Act) Rules 1989, r 18 and Family Proceedings Rules 1989, r 4.18.

- Obtain leave of the court for disclosure of necessary documents to the expert before sending them to the expert (see Family Proceedings Courts (Children Act) Rules 1989, r 23 and Family Proceedings Rules 1989, r 4.23) (provision of information or documents in a case without authority may be contempt of court – see *Practice Direction: Experts 2008* at 1.5).

- In emergency/urgent cases where there is insufficient time to obtain prior consent, the instructing party must apply forthwith on notice for directions as to the next steps regarding the expert (see *Practice Direction: Experts 2008* at 2.4).

*   Preliminary enquiries may be necessary in order to select the right expert. An approach to an expert should comply with *Practice Direction: Experts 2008* at 4.1-4.2. The instructing solicitor should then draft a proposed instruction in compliance with 4.3. and file it. Once it is agreed and leave is granted, it should be sent out within 5 days, 5.1.

*   Obtain consents from child and those with parental responsibility for examinations and assessments where appropriate (see Chapters 3 and 12 above).

*   Discuss instruction of expert with other parties and try to agree joint experts wherever possible.

*   The expert has an overriding duty to the court that takes precedence over the interests of any party, (see *Practice Direction: Experts 2008* at 3.1).

*   Directions of the court should be obtained for:

    (i) the date by which the letter of instruction should be sent;

    (ii) documents to be released;

    (iii) a date for filing the report.

*   Examination of a child may require directions as to venue, timing, the person(s) to accompany the child and to whom the results should be given.

Letters of instruction

Should comply with *Practice Direction: Experts 2008* at 5, in brief, to:

*   set out the context in which expert opinion sought;

*   define specific questions expert is to address;

*   list the documentation provided or refer to a paginated bundle;

*   identify materials that have not been produced either as original medical or other professional records or documents filed in response to an instruction from a party;

*   identify all requests to third parties for information and responses;

*   identify all the people concerned with the proceedings, informing he expert of their right to talk to them provided than an accurate record is made of discussions;

- identify any other expert instructed;

- define the contractual basis upon which the expert is instructed, including funding and payment details.

Letters of instruction should also be accompanied by a chronology with the background information, and request the expert to ask for further information or documentation if necessary.

The letter should then be filed at court with list of accompanying documents, and served on other parties unless the court otherwise directs.

Joint instructions are desirable, but not compulsory, see *Re CB and JB (Care Proceedings: Guidelines)* [1998] 2 FLR 211. Where letters of instruction are to be settled the procedure by email is set out in *Practice Direction: Experts 2008* at 5.2.

Updating, expert conferences, agreed evidence and points in issue

- Experts should be kept up to date with new documents filed in the case. *Practice Direction: Experts 2008* at 5.3.

- Experts may be invited to confer together, identifying areas of agreement and disputed issues. The court should regulate such meetings. *Practice Direction: Experts 2008* at 6.2-6.5.

Experts' Reports

- Expert reports should be objective – the expert's overriding duty is to the court.

- Parties and lawyers should not attempt to influence or 'edit' expert reports.

- Reports must be disclosed to the court; and to all parties unless otherwise directed by the court.

- The requirements for the content and ordering of an expert's report are set out in *Practice Direction: Experts 2008* at 3.3.

- The report shall end with statements that:

  (i) The expert understands his duty to the court and will comply with it;

  (ii) The expert does not consider that there is any conflict of interest, nor any interest disclosed that affects his suitability as an expert witness. He will advise those instructing him if there is any change in circumstances affecting his answers regarding interests and suitability.

- The report shall end with a statement of truth as follows:

  I confirm that insofar as the facts stated in my report are within my own knowledge I have made clear which they are and I believe them to be true, and that the opinions I have expressed represent my true and complete professional opinion. (*Practice Direction: Experts 2008* at 3.3.(13)).

18.2 Expert evidence in court

With careful planning by advocates, the time and patience of expert witnesses can be saved considerably. Joint consultations and jointly compiled experts' lists of agreed and disputed issues save time, whilst arrangement of evidence in a logical sequence to fit the needs of witnesses and the run of the evidence is vital. Written evidence can be admitted by agreement, and expert witnesses' time saved by reduction of their evidence in chief and more time in cross examination.

In the Civil Procedure Rules 1998, part 35 the primary duty of an expert is stated to be to the court. Although it was the expectation of the courts, this duty did not specifically apply in family cases until 1 April 2008, when the *Practice Direction: Experts in Family Proceedings Relating to Children. 13 February, 2008* (EFPRC 2008) para 3.1 came into effect. Now, that duty is very clearly stated.

Experts should never go beyond the remit of their instructions or their expertise. There have been cases in which, regrettably, this has happened, to the detriment of a party, the child, justice, or possibly all three. The Court of Appeal gave helpful guidance for experts and lawyers in *R v Cannings* [2004] EWCA Crim 1 [2004] 1 WLR 2607.

18.3 Finances for expert evidence

Under *The Practice Direction: Experts in Family Proceedings Relating to Children. 13 February, 2008* (EFPRC 2008 para 2.1) the contractual basis for the expert evidence, including funding and payment, should be set out in the letter of instruction.

Private funding is a matter of negotiation between client, solicitor and expert.

In publicly funded cases, the Legal Services Commission places limitations on funding. High cost cases (lawyers are advised to check the current limit) are dealt with by the Special Cases Unit and the lawyer needs to present and justify an overall cost case plan.

Careful negotiation of expert fees is required in advance of the case to obtain prior authority for instruction of the expert.

Any additional unforeseen expense in respect of the expert's assessment or report preparation which arises after the initial authority must be addressed by an increase in any limitation on costs that has been imposed by the Legal Services Commission.

Experts in publicly funded cases would be wise to accept instructions and begin work only when their fee structure, an estimate of their costs, and the responsibility for who will pay, along with an agreement as to how and when payment will be made has been clarified. This contractual arrangement should be reflected in the letter of instruction, *Practice Direction: Experts 2008* at 2.1.

When the expert's evidence or other work is concluded, claims for Payment on Account for expert services can be submitted to the Legal Services Commission in advance of the final detailed assessment of the costs of the case (formerly called taxation).

Experts should be aware that, if the matter is publicly funded, in county court or High Court cases, the detailed assessment (new form of taxation) may, in some circumstances, lead to a reduction in the fees allowed for the expert's work.

18.4 Finding the right expert

The most effective way of finding experts is by personal recommendation by other legal practitioners in similar fields of practice. CAFCASS, children's guardians, social workers, local authority lawyers, and other professionals may also provide recommendations for experts in particular specialist areas. Ask expert(s) to disclose qualifications, current work and relevant past experience – not only for reassurance, but also because to do so is useful for the court, other parties and the Legal Services Commission. Ask how often the expert has given evidence in court before – they may be absolutely brilliant on paper, but terrible at giving oral evidence.

The list of registers and directories below may be a starting point in the search for the right expert.

18.4.1 Experts lists, registers and directories

Some of these organisations will send out published lists. Others provide information in response to a telephone or written enquiry, and may charge an administration fee.

Organisation	*Title*
British Psychological Society	*Directory of Chartered Psychologists*
The Forensic Science Society	*World List of Forensic Science Laboratories and Practices*
The Forensic Science Society	*Register of Independent Consultants*
JS Publications	*UK Register of Expert Witnesses*
Law Society	*Expert Witness Register*
Law Society of Scotland	*Directory of Expert Witnesses*
British Academy of Experts	*Register of Experts*

Online resources to find experts

Directory of Expert Witnesses (Psychologists) http://www.bps.org.uk/e-services/find-a-psychologist/expertwitness.cfm

The Expert Witness website http://www.expertwitness.co.uk/

The Expert Witness Directory http://www.legalhub.co.uk/

The Directory of Expert Witnesses http://www.expertwitnessscotland.info/

UK Register of Expert Witnesses http://www.jspubs.com/

Journals and supplements

Expert Evidence, (International Digest of Human Behaviour, Science and Law) SLE Publications

Solicitors Journal, Expert Witnesses Supplement
Law Society Gazette, Expert Witness Supplement

Lawyers' lists

Law Society's Children Panel Membership List
London Criminal Courts Solicitors Association Agency and Membership List
Association of Lawyers for Children Experts Database

Useful information on instructing experts

Children Act Advisory Committee, (1997) *Handbook of Best Practice in Children Act Cases*, London: HMSO/DoH

Cowan, S & Hunt, AC (2008) *Mason's Forensic Medicine for Lawyers*, 5th edition, Haywards Heath: Tottel

Expert Witness Group, (1997) *Expert Witness Pack for Use in Children Act Proceedings*, Bristol: Family Law

Hodgkinson, T, and James, M (2006), *Expert Evidence Law and Practice*, 2nd edition, London: Sweet & Maxwell

Kennedy, I and Grubb, A (2000) *Medical Law: Text with Materials*, 3rd edition, Oxford: Oxford University Press

Wall, N. Justice & Hamilton, I (2007) *A Handbook for Expert Witnesses in Children Act Cases*, 2nd edition, Bristol: Family Law

19 Information, Guidance and Reference Works

19.1 The child protection practitioner's essential information library

Practitioners often ask us to list the basic essentials for child protection practice. The reference works listed below will provide an adequate reference library with which to start.. Many of the items listed are available online, and all are listed in full in sections 19.2 to 19.6, below.

> *The Children Act 1989 Guidance and Regulations* comprising Volumes 1- 10
> *Assessing Children in Need and their Families* (2000)
> *Framework for the Assessment of Children in Need and their Families* (2000)
> *Family Assessment Pack of Questionnaires and Scales* (2000)
> *Initial and Core Assessment Records* (2000)
> *Every Child Matters* (2004)
> *Family Law Protocol* (2006)
> *Introduction to the Children Act 1989* (1991)
> *Report of the Inquiry into Child Abuse in Cleveland,* (1987)
> *Representation of Children in Public Law Proceedings* (2006)
> *The Care of Children, Principles and Practice in Regulations and Guidance* (1991)
> *The Children Act Advisory Committee Handbook of Best Practice in Children Act Cases* (1997)
> *The SFLA Guide to Good Practice for Solicitors Acting for Children* (2002)
> *The Public Law Outline (PLO), issued as Practice Direction: Guide to Case Management in Public Law Proceedings*
> *President's Guidance: Adoption Proceedings. Intercountry Adoption Centres* (2007)
> *President's Guidance: The Private Law Programme* (2004)
>
> *Working Together to Safeguard Children* (2006)
>
> - Home Office Circular 88/1982
> - Home Office Circular 105/1982
> - Home Office Circular 102/1988
> - Home Office Circular 45/1991
> - Local Authority Circular LAC (1988) 20
> - Local Authority Circular LAC (1998) 29

- Local Authority Circular LAC (1999) 29

Family Bench Book and the *Family Training Pack*

Practitioners in Scotland should have all the Scottish resources listed in 19.7 below.

19.1.2   Additional resources

In addition to the resources listed above, child law practitioners should have access to:

A child and family law reference work, regularly updated (see 19.2 below)

An up to date book on child development (see 19.2 below)

Family/child law reports

Family/child law journals/newsletters

Sample set of *Centile Charts for baby growth*, with accompanying explanatory notes (obtainable from a GP or Health Visitor or http://www.gp-training.net)

List(s) of expert witnesses

Local Safeguarding Children Board Manual (formerly the *ACPC Local Manual*. If available, usually obtainable from the LSCB Chair, there may be a fee payable)

Children Act Advisory Committee Handbook of Best Practice: Directions, Pro Formas, Public and Private Law, available at www.dhsspsni.gov.uk/child_advisory_bestpractice.pdf

Memorandum of Good Practice in Video Recorded Interviews of Children, (1992)

Interviewing Child Witnesses under the Memorandum of Good Practice (1999)

UN Convention on the Rights of the Child 1992

European Convention for the Protection of Human Rights and Fundamental Freedoms (1950) and the Protocols made under it.

19.2   Sources: statutes

- Abortion Act 1967
- Access to Health Records Act 1990

- Access to Medical Reports Act 1988
- Access to Justice Act 1999
- Adoption and Children Act 2002
- Adoption and Children (Scotland) Act 2007
- Care Standards Act 2000
- Carers and Disabled Children Act 2000
- Child Abduction Act 1984
- Child Abduction and Custody Act 1985
- Child Support Act 1991
- Children Act 2004
- Children Act 1989
- Children (Leaving Care) Act 2000
- Children and Adoption Act 2006
- Children and Young Persons Act 1933
- Children and Young Persons Act 1969
- Children (Scotland) Act 1995
- Commissioner for Children and Young People (Scotland) Act 2003
- County Courts Act 1984
- Crime and Disorder Act 1998
- Data Protection Act 1988
- Domestic Proceedings and Magistrates' Courts Act 1978
- Domicile and Matrimonial Proceedings Act 1973
- Education Act 2002
- Family Law Act 1986
- Family Law Act 1996
- Family Law Reform Act 1969
- Family Law Reform Act 1987
- Foster Children Act 1980
- Human Fertilisation and Embryology Act 1990

- Human Rights Act 1998
- Local Authority Social Services Act 1970
- Mental Capacity Act 2005
- Mental Health Act 1983
- Police and Criminal Evidence Act 1984
- Protection from Harassment Act 1997
- Protection of Children Act 1999
- Race Relations Act 1976
- Rehabilitation of Offenders Act 1974
- Sexual Offences Act 1956
- Sexual Offences Act 2003
- Supreme Court Act 1981
- Surrogacy Arrangements Act 1985

19.3   Sources: statutory instruments

- Access to Justice (Destination of Appeals) (Family Proceedings) Order 2009, SI 2009/871.
- Access to Personal Files (Social Services) Regulations 1989, SI 1989/206
- Access to Personal Files (Social Services) (Amendment) Regulations 1991, SI 1991/1587
- Adoption Support Agencies (England) and Adoption Agencies (Miscellaneous Amendments) Regulations 2005, SI 2005/2720
- Adoption Agencies Regulations 2005, SI 2005/389
- Adoption Agencies (Wales) Regulations 2005, SI 2005/1313
- Adoption (Bringing Children into the United Kingdom) Regulations 2003, SI 2003 /1173
- Adoption Information and Intermediary Services Regulations (pre-commencement) 2005, SI 2005/890
- Adoption Support Services Regulations 2005, SI 2005/691
- Adoptions with a Foreign Element Regulations 2005, SI 2002 /392

- Arrangements for Placement of Children (General) Regulations 1991, SI 1991/890

- The Allocation and Transfer of Proceedings Order 2008, SI 2008/28

- Blood Tests (Evidence of Paternity) Regulations 1971, SI 1971/1861

- Children Act 2004 Information Data Base [England] Regulations 2007, SI 2007/2182

- Care Homes Regulations 2001, SI 2001/3965

- Child Minding and Day Care (Applications for Registration) (England) Regulations 2001, SI 2002/1829

- Child Minding and Day Care (Applications for Registration) (England) Regulations 2001, SI 2001/1829

- Child Minding and Day Care (Certificates of Registration) (England) Regulations 2001, SI 2001/1830

- Child Minding and Day Care (Suspension of Registration) (England) Regulations 2003, SI 2003/332

- Children Act 2004 (Children's Services) Regulations 2005, SI 2005/1972.

- Children (Allocation of Proceedings) Order 1991, SI 1991/1677

- Children (Allocation of Proceedings, Appeals) Order 1991, SI 1991/1801

- Children (Allocation of Proceedings, Amendment) Orders 1994, 1997 and 1998

- Children and Family Court Advisory and Support Service (Conduct of Litigation and Exercise of Rights of Audience) Regulations 2001, SI 2001/669

- Children (Leaving Care) (England) Regulations 2001, SI 2001/2874

- Children (Leaving Care) (Wales) Regulations 2001, SI 2001/2189

- Children (Private Arrangements for Fostering) Regulations 2005, SI 2005/1533

- Children (Private Arrangements for Fostering) (Wales) Regulations 2006, SI 2006/940

- Children (Secure Accommodation) Regulations 1991, SI 1991/1505

- Children (Secure Accommodation No 2) Regulations 1991, SI 1991/2034

- Children (Admissibility of Hearsay Evidence) Order 1993, SI 1993/621

- Civil Procedure Rules 1998, SI 1998/3132

- Community Legal Service (Financial Regulations) 2000, SI 2000/516

- Community Legal Service (Cost Protection) Regulations 2000, SI 2000/824

- Community Legal Service (Costs) Regulations 2000, SI 2000/441

- Contact with Children Regulations 1991, SI 1991/891

- County Court Rules 1981, SI 1981/1687

- Court of Protection Rules 2007, SI 2007/1744

- Data Protection (Processing of Sensitive Personal Data) Order 2000

- Data Protection (Subject Access Modification) Order 2000

- Disclosure of Adoption Information (post-commencement adoptions) 2005, SI 2005/888

- Disqualification from Caring for Children Regulations 2002, SI 2002/635

- Family Law Act 1996 (Part IV) (Allocation of Proceedings) Order 1997, SI 1997/1896

- Family Proceedings Courts (Children Act 1989) Rules 1991, SI 1991/1395

- Family Proceedings Rules 1991, SI 1991/1247

- Family Procure (Adoption) Rules 2005, SI 2005/2795

- Foster Placement (Children) Regulations 1991, SI 1991/910

- Fostering Services Regulations 2002, SI 2002/57

- Guardians ad Litem and Reporting Officers (Panels) (Amendment) Regulations 1997, SI 1997/1662

- Parental Responsibility Agreement Regulations 1991, SI 1991/1478

- Parental Responsibility Agreement (Amendment) Regulations 1994, SI 1994 /3157

- Placement of Children with Parents etc Regulations 1991, SI 1991/893

- Representations Procedure (Children) Regulations 1991, SI 1991/894

- Review of Childrens' Cases Regulations 1991, SI 1991/895

- Rules of the Supreme Court 1965, SI 1965/1776

- Special Guardianship Regulations 2005, SI 2005/1109

- Special Guardianship (Wales) Regulations 2005, SI 2005/1513

- Suitability of Adopters Regulations 2005, SI 2002/1712

19.4   Sources: conventions and protocols

- UN Convention on the Rights of the Child (in force in the UK on 15 January 1992)

- European Convention for the Protection of Human Rights and Fundamental Freedoms

- Protocols made under the European Convention for the Protection of Human Rights and Fundamental Freedoms

19.5   Sources: practice directions

The Public Law Outline (PLO) issued as *Practice Direction: Guide to Case Management in Public Law Proceedings* [2008] available at www.justice.gov. uk/guidance/careproceedings.htm

President's Guidance: Adoption Proceedings. Intercountry Adoption Centres (2007)

President's Guidance: The Private Law Programme (2004)

Adopted Children Register: Restriction on Disclosure [1999] 1 FLR 315

Children Act 1989 Applications by Children [1993] 1 FLR 1008 available at www.justice.gov.uk/guidance/careproceedings.htm

President's Guidance: Adoption Proceedings. Intercountry Adoption Centres (2008)

President's Guidance Adoption: The New Law and Procedure available at http://www.judiciary.gov.uk/docs/adoption_final.pdf

Practice Direction – Allocation and Transfer of Proceedings available at http://www.judiciary.gov.uk/docs/judgments_guidance/pd/practicedirection-on-allocation-final.pdf

19.6   Sources: practice guidance and government publications

British Government publications are available from The Stationery Office (TSO) www.tsoshop.co.uk. TSO, PO Box 29, Norwich, NR3 1GN, Tel: 0870 600 5522, E-mail: customer.services@tso.co.uk. Guidance is available at www.justice.gov.uk/guidance/careproceedings.htm.

The Scottish Office and The Scottish Executive publications are available at available at www.scotland.gov.uk. See also the Scottish Courts http:// www.scotcourts.gov.uk/

For the National Assembly for Wales, see www.wales.gov.uk.

The Children Act 1989: Guidance and Regulations comprising:

> Volume 1 Court Orders (England) revised 2008
> Volume 1 Court Orders (Wales) 2008
> Volume 2 Family Support, Day Care, and Educational Provision for Young Children
> Volume 3 Family Placements
> Volume 4 Residential Care
> Volume 5 Independent Schools
> Volume 6 Children with Disabilities
> Volume 7 Guardians ad Litem and Other Court Related Issues
> Volume 8 Private Fostering and Miscellaneous
> Volume 9 Adoption Issues
> Volume 10 Index

Assessing Children in Need and their Families (2000)

The Care of Children, Principles and Practice in Regulations and Guidance (1991)

Every Child Matters: Change for Children (2004) www.everychildmatters.gov.uk

Family Assessment Pack of Questionnaires and Scales (2000); *Framework for the Assessment of Children in Need and their Families* (2000); *Family Assessment Pack of Questionnaires and Scales* (2000) and *Initial and Core Assessment Records* (2000) All available online at www.ecm.gov.uk/caf

Family Bench Book and the Family Training Pack available from http://www.jsboard.co.uk/family_law/index.htm or Publications Co-Ordinator, The Judicial Studies Board, 9th Floor, Millbank Tower, Millbank, London, SW1P 4QU

Family Law Protocol (2006) The Law Society

Guide to Listing Officers (Lord Chancellor's Department, September 1991)

Information Sharing - A Practitioner's Guide (2006)

Introduction to the Children Act 1989 (1991)

Report of the Inquiry into Child Abuse in Cleveland (1987)

Representation of Children in Public Law Proceedings, The Law Society's Guidance (2006)

The Right to Complain (1991)

The Children Act Advisory Committee Handbook of Best Practice in Children Act Cases 1997

The Protection of Children in England: A Progress Report (Lord Laming, 12 March 2009)

The SFLA Guide to Good Practice for Solicitors Acting for Children (2002)

The Victoria Climbé Inquiry: Report (Lord Laming, 28 Jan 2003)

What to do if You are Worried a Child is being Abused (2006)

Working Together to Safeguard Children (2006)

Scotland

Scottish Executive (2006) *Getting it Right for Every Child*

Scottish Executive (2004a) *Protecting Children and Young People: The Charter, Edinburgh, Scottish Executive*

Scottish Executive (2004b) *Protecting Children and Young People: The Framework for Standards, Edinburgh, Scottish Executive*

Scottish Executive (2003a) *Sharing Information about Children at Risk*

Scottish Executive (2003b) *"It's Everyone's Job to Make Sure I'm Alright": Report of the Child Protection Audit and Review: Edinburgh: Scottish Executive*

Scottish Executive (2003c) *Framework for Standards and Children's Charter*

Scottish Executive (2002) *Getting our Priorities Right*

The Scottish Office (1998a) *Protecting Children – A shared responsibility. Guidance on Inter-Agency Co-operation.*

The Scottish Office (1998b) *Protecting Children – A shared responsibility. Guidance for Health Professionals in Scotland*

19.7   Sources: Home Office and Local Authority Circulars

* Home Office Circular 88/1982
* Home Office Circular 105/1982
* Home Office Circular 102/1988
* Home Office Circular 45/1991
* Local Authority Circular LAC (1988) 20
* Local Authority Circular LAC (1998) 29
* Local Authority Circular LAC (1999) 29

19.8   Reading and reference list

These publications have been recommended by practitioners as useful resource material for child law practitioners in addition to the basic reference library listed in 19.1 above. We welcome suggestions for new publications for inclusion in this list.

Loose-leaf reference works

Bromley, PM (ed), *The Family Law Service,* London: Butterworths

Hershman, D & McFarlane, Λ (eds), *Children Law and Practice,* Bristol: Family Law

Hoggett, B. (ed), *Clarke Hall and Morrison on Children,* London: Butterworths

Jones, RM (ed), *The Encyclopaedia of Social Services and Child Care Law,* London: Sweet & Maxwell

Child law books

Goldthorpe, L and Monro, P, (2005) *Child Law Handbook: Guide to good practice,* London: Law Society

Timms, JE, (2003) *Children's Representation, A Practitioner's Guide,* London: Sweet & Maxwell

Social work practice and assessments

Barker, J and Hodes, D, (2007) *The Child in Mind: A Child Protection Handbook,* 3rd edition, Abingdon: Routledge

Brandon, M, Belderson, P, et al (2008) *Analysing Child Deaths and Serious Injury through Abuse and Neglect: What can we Learn? – A Biennial Analysis of*

Serious Case Reviews 2003 – 2005, London: Department for Children, Schools and Families

Calder, MC (2008) *Contemporary Risk Assessment in Safeguarding Children,* Lyme Regis: Russell House

Commission for Social Care Inspection (2005) *Safeguarding Children – The Second Joint Chief Inspectors' Report on Arrangements to Safeguard Children,* Norwich: TSO

Reder, P, Duncan, S & Gray, M, (1993) *Beyond Blame,* London: Routledge

Rose, W & Barnes, J (2008) *Improving Safeguarding Practice – Study of Serious Case Reviews 2001 – 2003,* London: Department for Children, Schools and Families

Forensic work in children cases

Dent, H & Flynn, R. (eds) (1996), *Children as Witnesses,* Chichester: Wiley

Meadow, R., Mok, J, & Rosenberg, D (eds), (2007) *ABC of Child Protection,* London: BMJ

Memorandum of Good Practice in Interviewing Child Witnesses (1991), Norwich: TSO

Davies, G & Westcott, H (1999) *Interviewing Child Witnesses under the Memorandum of Good Practice*

Police Research Paper 115 at www.homeoffice.gov.uk/rds/prgpdfs/fprs115.pdf

Child development

Charlesworth, R (2003) *Understanding Child Development,* London: Delmar Learning

Hobart, C. & Frankel, J (2004) *A Practical Guide to Child Observation and Assessment,* London: Nelson Thornes

Holt, K S (1994) *Child Development — Diagnosis and Assessment,* London: Butterworth

Megitt, C (2006) *Child Development: An Illustrated Guide,* 2nd edition, London: Heinemann

Useful information

Department of Health and Social Services Inspectorate (1991) *The Right to Complain*, London: HMSO

Expert Witness Group (1997) *Expert Witness Pack for Use in Children Act Proceedings*, Bristol: Family Law

Farmer, R & Moyers, S (2008) *Kinship Care: Fostering Effective Family and Friends Placements*, London: Jessica Kingsley

Friel, J (1997) *Children with Special Needs*, 4th edition, London: Jessica Kingsley

Hunt, J, Waterhouse, S, & Lutman, E (2008) *Keeping Them in the Family: Outcomes for children placed in kinship care through care proceedings*, London: BAAF

Isaacs, E & Shepherd, C (2008) *Social Work Decision Making: A guide for child care lawyers*, Bristol: Family Law

Mahendra, B (2008) *Risk Assessment in Psychiatry*, Bristol: Family Law

Pressdee, P, Vater, J, Judd, F and Baker, J (2008) *The Public Law Outline: The Court Companion*. Bristol, Family Law.

Valman, HB (1999) *ABC of One to Seven*, 4th edition, London: BMJ

Valman, HB (1997) *Children's Medical Guide*, London: Dorling Kindersley Publishing

Wall, Justice (ed) (1997) *Rooted Sorrows*, Bristol: Family Law

Wall, Justice & Hamilton, I (2007) *Handbook for Expert Witnesses in Children Act Cases*, 2nd edition, Bristol: Family Law

Specialist law updates and online resources

Practitioner's Guide to Child Law Remy Zentar (ed), available from:

24 Rathen Road
Withington
Manchester M20 9GH

http://www.practitionersguides.co.uk/contact.html

Family Law Reports	Jordans, Family Law www.familylaw.co.uk/
Solicitors Family Law Directory	www.familylawdirectory.co.uk/
Justis (online resource)	www.justis.com

UK Statute law   www.statutelaw.gov.uk/

UK Statutory Instruments   www.opsi.gov.uk/stat.htm

Scottish Statutory Instruments   www.opsi.gov.uk/legislation/scotland/s-stat.htm

TSO on-line bookshop   http://www.tsoshop.co.uk/

20 Improving Law, Skills and Practice

It is necessary for lawyers to keep up to date with statute and case law and to constantly develop knowledge and skills, not only in law but, for example, in medicine, psychology and parenting.

Look for training events which are accredited by the Solicitors Regulation Authority (courses which were formerly accredited by the Law Society), the Bar Council, or the Family Mediation Council and those run by the associations listed below at 20.1.

It is vital to maintain a list of resources to which child clients and families may be referred and it helps to belong to organisations which can provide information and assistance. In those areas of the country where child law practitioners may find themselves isolated, discussion with a network of colleagues provides moral and practical support.

20.1 Professional and interdisciplinary associations

A good resource for child law practice is the experience of colleagues. Listed below are some of the organisations which have been recommended to us as helpful in the provision of networking, training and information. By listing these, we are not expressing any preference, and the list is by no means exhaustive.

Association of Lawyers for Children
The Administrator PO Box 283, East Molesey, KT8 OWH
www.alc.org.uk admin@alc.org.uk

British Association for Adoption and Fostering
Secretary , Saffron House, 6-10 Kirby Street, London EC1N 8TS
Tel: 020 7421 2600 Fax: 020 7421 2601
www.baaf.org.uk mail@baaf.org.uk

British Association for the Study and Prevention of Child Abuse and Neglect (BASPCAN)
National Administrator 17 Priory Street, York YO1 6ET
Tel: 01904 613605 Fax: 01904 642239
baspcan@baspcan.org.uk

The Children and Family Court Advisory and Support Service (CAFCASS)
8th Floor, South Quay Plaza 3, 189 Marsh Wall, London, E 14 9SH
Tel 020 7510 7000 Fax 020 7510 7001
www.cafcass.gov.uk email: webenquiries@cafcass.gov.uk

The Family Justice Council www.family-justice-council.org.uk

Judicial Studies Board http://www.jsboard.co.uk

Local Children's Guardian and Solicitor Groups
Check with local CAFCASS Managers

NAGALRO (National Association for Guardians ad Litem and Reporting Officers)
PO Box 264, Esher, Surrey, KT10 OWA
www.nagalro.com   Email nagalro@globalnet.co.uk
Note: NAGALRO has a great GOOGLE group for Practitioners-membership is available to child and family lawyers.

National Youth Advisory Service
Egerton House, Tower Road, Birkenhead, Wirral, CH41 1FN
Tel: 0151 649 8700 Fax: 0151 649 8701
www.nyas.net nyas@charity.vfree.com

Resolution
Secretary, PO Box 302, Orpington, Kent BR6 8QX
Tel: 01689 820272 Fax: 01689 896972
www.resolution.org.uk Email info@resolution.org.uk

20.2 The Law Society's Children Panel

The Children Panel comprises practitioners specialising in the representation of children, families and local authorities in public or private law matters.

For membership, applicants must have post-qualification experience in child and family law and a sound knowledge of child law and practice. In addition, they need an understanding of child related issues, for example, child development, attachment and separation, recognition of child abuse, contact and care planning. They also develop their skills in communicating with children.

Solicitors wishing to be accepted for membership of the Children Panel must produce evidence of the appropriate qualifications and relevant experience; provide references; acquire the necessary training; and, on application, will be asked to submit written answers to questions. Finally, they must pass a selection interview.

Children Panel training courses are comprehensive, covering a wide range of topics and law relevant to the representation of children, families and local authorities and working with the children's guardian.

Information about the Children Panel and application forms can be obtained from   The Solicitors Regulation Authority, Ipsley Court, Berrington Close, Redditch, Worcestershire B98 OTD. DZ 19114 Redditch. Website: www.accreditation.sra.org.uk. Email contactcentre@sra.org.uk.

http://www.sra.org.uk/solicitors/accreditation/children-panel-accreditation-scheme.page